COOKING WITH
Bon Appétit

COOKING WITH
Bon Appétit

Light
Desserts

THE KNAPP PRESS
Publishers
Los Angeles

Copyright © 1984 by Knapp Communications Corporation

Published by The Knapp Press
5900 Wilshire Boulevard, Los Angeles, California 90036

Library of Congress Cataloging in Publication Data

Main entry under title:

Light desserts.

(Cooking with Bon appétit)
Includes index.
1. Desserts. I. Bon appétit. II. Series.
TX773.L485 1984   641.8'6   83-24876
ISBN 0-89535-135-8

On the cover: *Fresh Strawberry Sorbet*

Printed and bound in the United States of America
10 9 8 7 6 5 4 3 2

❦ Contents

❦ *Foreword*

====================

"To me, the best desserts are light, sort of transparent, in that they don't obliterate the dishes that precede them," says the recognized "Dean of American Cooking" in his recent best-seller, *The New James Beard*. We heartily agree. And that is why we've put together this superb collection of recipes from the pages of *Bon Appétit*. All of them have two delightful things in common—they are light, fresh and flavorful, fitting perfectly into today's lighter style of eating. And they are not heavy or filling—ideal finishes for any meal from a bountiful holiday party to a casual dinner for friends or family.

But light does not mean lackluster, as you'll discover in these exciting recipes. There are wonderful feasts for the eye and the palate, such as Persimmon Soufflé Roll (page 58), Toasted Almond-Snow Ice Cream in Pineapple Boats (page 93) and Frozen Strawberry Mousse in a Meringue Shell (page 47). Reflecting the wide variety of light desserts, the recipes are organized into five chapters: Fruit Desserts, Mousses, Soufflés, Iced Desserts (sorbets, sherbets, ices and ice creams) and Cookies. The recipes incorporate ideas from just about every corner of the globe as well as the best from right here at home. We have also included some helpful tips and techniques to ensure success every step of the way, including what to look for when creating your own fruit and cheese dessert combinations, mastering the art of those sometimes-tricky soufflés and dessert omelets and a simple guide to some wonderful light *alternatives* to dessert—the wide array of dessert liqueurs.

For the contemporary dessert lover, it's an ideal companion. And you will still find all of your old favorites—chocolate, berries, lemon, nuts and caramel among them—but all in great new guises that are fanciful, distinctive and sublime.

1 ❦ Fruit Desserts

Adam's fall is generally depicted as having been caused by biting into an apple. This may make sense to ecclesiastical scholars and students of allegory, but to dessert lovers it is more than a little mysterious. After all, what could be more innocent than a piece of fruit? What could be more pure? And, more to the gastronomic point, what could be so *good*? Light and refreshing fresh fruit, with its natural sweetness, appealing color and great nutritive value, is perhaps the most perfect of all dessert foods—and no matter how it is dressed up, it is about as far from a fall from grace as you can get.

Fruits of every season are showcased in the desserts in this chapter. Peaches are filled with flavorful amaretto *zabaglione* or served up as an exceptionally easy *coupe* Melba. Pears are baked in a cider syrup or poached with a variety of flavorings: raspberry, almond and ginger cream. Apples are baked with Marsala and flamed with bourbon. Bright pineapple rings are enlivened with a gingered yogurt sauce, and this Hawaiian favorite also stars in a classic bavarian cream. Oranges lend color and tang to several new treats, and the exotic flavor of papaya is perfectly complemented by a sweet-sour raspberry and lime sauce. Strawberries, probably the most popular of all fruits, appear in fondant, as a sabayon and filled with cream. And, keeping in mind that the best flavoring for a fruit is often another fruit, there are a number of mixed fruit desserts here, too a sundae, a "fondue," a trio of delicious compotes and a spectacular mosaic of macaroon-stuffed fruits.

The variety of these desserts is matched only by their ease of preparation, and all of the recipes are designed to bring out the full flavor of the fruit. And—to return to Genesis for a moment—none of these desserts is exactly sinful, but all are most certainly original.

Marsala Baked Apples

4 servings

1 tablespoon golden raisins
1 tablespoon currants
4 teaspoons pine nuts, toasted, *or* slivered blanched almonds, toasted
Grated peel of 1 large lemon
4 medium Rome Beauty apples, cored
4 tablespoons Marsala

1 cup boiling water
2 tablespoons fresh lemon juice
2 teaspoons sugar

Preheat oven to 325°F. Mix raisins, currants, pine nuts and lemon peel. Fill apples evenly with mixture. Cut thin slit horizontally around middle of each apple to prevent bursting while cooking. Arrange apples upright in baking dish just large enough to hold fruit snugly. Drizzle 1 tablespoon Marsala into each filled hollow. Combine water and lemon juice, then pour mixture over apples. Cover apples with foil. Bake until tender, about 1 hour. Discard foil. Continue baking until apples are very soft and golden brown, basting frequently, about 20 more minutes; sprinkle sugar evenly over fruit during last 5 minutes (if raisins begin to brown, cover filling with small circle of foil). Transfer apples to individual dessert plates. Spoon over any juices remaining in baking dish. Serve apples warm or cool.

Bourbon Flamed Apples

This versatile dessert is delicious served with a dollop of sour cream or yogurt.

2 servings

2 large tart apples, cored, peeled, quartered and cut into ⅛-inch slices
1 tablespoon fresh lemon juice
2 tablespoons (¼ stick) unsalted butter
2 tablespoons firmly packed brown sugar

2 tablespoons warmed bourbon
Sour cream *or* plain yogurt *or* crème fraîche (see recipe, page 29)

Combine apple slices and lemon juice in bowl and toss gently. Melt butter in medium skillet over medium heat. Add apples and cook, turning frequently, until crisp-tender, about 10 minutes. Stir in brown sugar. Add bourbon and ignite, shaking skillet gently until flame subsides. Serve warm with desired accompaniment.

Currant-Apple Dessert

If serving dessert chilled, garnish with a dollop of sour cream.

2 servings

2 large tart green apples, peeled, cored and sliced
3 tablespoons brown sugar
1 tablespoon water
¼ teaspoon grated lemon peel

¼ teaspoon cinnamon
2 teaspoons currant jelly
⅛ teaspoon vanilla

Combine apples, sugar, water, lemon peel and cinnamon in medium skillet and toss thoroughly. Cover, place over medium heat and simmer gently 10 minutes. Add currant jelly and simmer, uncovered, 5 more minutes. Remove from heat and stir in vanilla. Serve hot or chilled.

Canton Apricots

4 to 6 servings

4 cups water
¾ cup sugar
1 pound whole fresh apricots
1 teaspoon cinnamon

Sauce
2 cups milk
1 cup sugar
1 teaspoon almond extract

Combine water and sugar in medium saucepan and bring to boil over high heat. Reduce heat, add apricots, cover and simmer until slightly soft, about 5 minutes. Stir in cinnamon. Cool and chill.

For sauce: Combine ingredients in small pan and bring to boil over medium heat. Cool and chill several hours or overnight. Serve over apricots.

Apricot Flambé

8 servings

24 dried apricots

¼ cup (½ stick) butter
¼ cup sugar
1 teaspoon fresh lemon juice

Pinch of salt
¼ cup white crème de cacao
¼ cup apricot brandy, warmed

Combine apricots in medium bowl with enough water to cover and let soak 8 hours or overnight.

Drain apricots well. Melt butter in large skillet over medium-high heat. Stir in apricots and sugar. Mix in lemon juice and salt and cook 5 to 10 minutes. Add crème de cacao and cook another 5 minutes. Pour warmed brandy over apricots and ignite, shaking pan gently until flame subsides. Transfer apricots to sauceboat and serve immediately.

Baked Bananas with Honey

4 servings

4 medium-small unpeeled bananas
4 teaspoons honey

1 large lime, quartered

Preheat oven to 350°F. Line baking dish with foil or parchment paper. Arrange bananas in prepared dish, spacing evenly. Bake until skins are golden brown and bananas feel soft, 20 to 30 minutes. Let cool 5 minutes. Make cut lengthwise through skin; open skin partially. Drizzle 1 teaspoon honey over each piece of fruit, then squeeze 1 lime wedge over each and serve.

Cassis Bavarois

A cool and delicious dessert from the menu of A La Côte St.-Jacques in Joigny, France.

8 servings

¾ cup sugar
½ cup plus 1 tablespoon milk
3 envelopes unflavored gelatin softened in about 5 tablespoons water
2 cups strained black currant (cassis) puree (about 3 cups fresh berries)

3 cups whipping cream
½ cup plus 2 tablespoons powdered sugar

Fresh black currants (garnish)

Combine sugar and milk in medium saucepan and bring to boil over medium-high heat. Add softened gelatin and blend well. Stir in cassis puree. Cool slightly; refrigerate until mixture is just beginning to set.

Combine 2¼ cups cream and ½ cup powdered sugar in large bowl of electric mixer. Stir at low speed until sugar is dissolved, then whip until cream holds soft peaks; *do not overbeat*. Gently fold cream into cassis mixture. Turn into 2-quart porcelain mold or soufflé dish. Chill until set, 6 hours.

To serve, unmold dessert onto platter. Whip remaining ¾ cup cream with remaining 2 tablespoons powdered sugar until soft peaks form. Spoon cream into pastry bag fitted with star tip. Pipe rosettes evenly around rim of dessert. Garnish rosettes with currants.

Blueberries with Lemon

12 servings

6 cups (3 pints) fresh blueberries, rinsed and drained
¼ to ⅓ cup sugar

1 teaspoon vanilla
1 teaspoon grated lemon peel

Gently mix all ingredients in medium bowl. Cover and chill overnight.

Cool Grape Dessert

4 servings

3 cups Thompson seedless grapes
2 cups sour cream
Juice of 2 limes
½ cup firmly packed brown sugar, or less if grapes are very sweet

1 tablespoon ground ginger, or to taste
1 lime cut into 4 wedges

Mix first 5 ingredients together. Chill thoroughly. Serve in chilled glass dishes with wedge of lime for each dish.

Melon Ambrosia Parfait

4 to 6 servings

1 6-ounce bottle ginger ale

1 medium cantaloupe, scooped into balls
1 cup shredded coconut
1 honeydew melon, scooped into balls

¼ large watermelon, scooped into balls (optional)

Fresh mint sprigs (garnish)

Pour ginger ale into ice cube trays and freeze until slushy but not solid.

Layer cantaloupe, coconut, honeydew and watermelon in parfait glasses. Refrigerate at least 1 hour.

Just before serving, top each parfait glass with scoop of slushy ginger ale and garnish with sprig of mint.

Fresh Melon with Herbed Mascarpone Sauce

6 servings

⅓ cup mascarpone cheese, room temperature
¼ cup fresh lime juice
2 tablespoons fresh lemon juice
½ small garlic clove, finely chopped
Salt and freshly ground pepper
2 tablespoons half and half
2 tablespoons mixed minced fresh herbs (parsley, basil, mint, rosemary, oregano)

1 cup (about) olive oil

1 cantaloupe
½ honeydew melon
½ crenshaw melon
2 limes, peeled and segmented (garnish)
6 fresh mint sprigs (garnish)

Blend mascarpone, lime and lemon juices in medium bowl. Mash garlic to puree; add to cheese. Add salt and pepper. Whisk in half and half until smooth. Blend in herbs. Gradually whisk in oil in slow steady stream until mixture is saucelike consistency. Taste and adjust seasoning. *(Mixture may be prepared ahead to this point, covered with plastic wrap and refrigerated. Bring mixture to room temperature and rewhisk before using.)*

Spoon out melon balls using different sized scoops (you should have about 6 cups). Arrange in stemmed glasses. Pour some of sauce over. Garnish with lime and mint. Pass remaining sauce separately.

Marinated Citrus with Cheese Zabaglione

6 servings

3 oranges
1 lemon
1 lime
3 tablespoons dry Marsala
1 tablespoon superfine sugar

6 egg yolks, room temperature
½ cup sugar

½ cup dry Marsala mixed with 1 tablespoon vanilla extract
1 tablespoon freshly grated Parmesan cheese
1 tablespoon finely chopped or crumbled Gorgonzola cheese

Peel citrus fruits, removing all white pith. Slice fruits into ¼-inch rounds. Remove center core and seeds. Arrange slices alternately in broilerproof dish. Sprinkle with 3 tablespoons Marsala and sugar. Cover with plastic wrap and refrigerate at least several hours or overnight.

Preheat broiler. Drain marinade into heavy large saucepan. Add yolks and sugar and whisk until pale yellow and creamy, about 5 minutes. Set over slightly larger pan of gently simmering water. Slowly add Marsala mixed with vanilla, beating constantly until mixture forms soft mounds; do not boil. Remove from heat. Blend in cheeses. Spoon over fruit slices. Broil until brown and bubbly. Serve.

Snow of Gingered Citrus

After blending, this pretty dessert layers into a light amber-colored jelly at the bottom with a crown of puffy egg white. Show it off in your favorite clear glass or crystal serving dish.

8 to 10 servings

½ cup fresh orange juice
¼ cup fresh lemon juice
4 teaspoons unflavored gelatin

3 cups dry white wine
½ cup sugar
4 heaping tablespoons fine julienne of orange peel (colored part only)
4 heaping teaspoons fine julienne of lemon peel (colored part only)

4 teaspoons preserved ginger syrup
2 heaping teaspoons minced drained preserved ginger in syrup*

10 egg whites, room temperature
¼ teaspoon cream of tartar
Pinch of salt
¼ cup sugar

Blend orange and lemon juices in small bowl. Sprinkle with gelatin.

Cook white wine, ½ cup sugar and citrus peels in heavy saucepan over low heat until sugar dissolves, swirling pan occasionally. Increase heat and boil 6 minutes. Remove from heat and stir in ginger syrup, minced ginger and gelatin mixture until gelatin dissolves completely. Cool to room temperature, stirring frequently, about 1 hour. Do not allow mixture to set.

Stir gelatin mixture with wooden spatula to loosen any gelatin settled at bottom. Beat whites in large bowl with cream of tartar and salt until soft peaks form. Gradually sprinkle with sugar and continue beating until whites are stiff but not dry. Using large rubber spatula, push aside some of whites and pour gelatin mixture down side of bowl. Fold liquid into whites just until blended. Turn into 3-quart glass serving bowl. Use tip of spatula to lift up peaks of whites to decorate top. Cover with plastic and refrigerate at least 8 hours or overnight.

*Available at specialty foods stores.

Oranges with Ginger and White Wine

8 servings

10 navel oranges

1⅓ cups dry white wine
1 10-ounce jar preserved ginger in syrup, undrained

1 cup fresh orange juice
2 tablespoons fresh lemon juice
1½ tablespoons superfine sugar

¼ cup diced candied ginger

Remove zest from 2 oranges using vegetable peeler. Cut into thinnest possible julienne. Wrap peel tightly in foil or plastic and refrigerate. Peel all oranges, removing the white membrane. Slice thinly. Transfer orange slices to serving bowl.

Combine wine, preserved ginger (with syrup), orange and lemon juices, and sugar in processor or blender and mix using on/off turns until ginger is finely chopped. Pour over orange slices and toss gently. Cover and refrigerate at least 4 hours (or up to 24).

Just before serving, baste orange slices with wine mixture. Sprinkle with reserved orange peel julienne and ¼ cup diced candied ginger.

Orange Fantasia

10 servings

8 to 9 large navel oranges

2 cups sugar
1 cup water

5 tablespoons Grand Marnier

1 cup whipping cream
2 tablespoons powdered sugar
½ teaspoon vanilla
½ cup slivered almonds, toasted

Using peeler or stripper, remove peel from oranges. Cut julienne and set aside. Remove and discard pith. Separate oranges into segments. Cut each in half, remove seeds and transfer to mixing bowl.

Combine sugar and water in small saucepan and stir until sugar is dissolved. Let boil without stirring 5 minutes. Remove from heat and cool.

Add liqueur to orange segments and toss lightly. Blend in ¼ cup cooled syrup and stir to coat evenly.

Lightly oil baking sheet. Return remaining syrup to boil, add orange peel and boil slowly 5 minutes. Remove peel with slotted spoon and spread on prepared baking sheet to cool.

Divide orange segments among serving dishes. Whip cream with powdered sugar and vanilla until stiff. Top oranges with generous dollop of cream and sprinkle with nuts and orange peel.

Oranges Orientale

There aren't many desserts that provide the perfect finale to a Chinese meal, but this is one. When you're frantically juggling ingredients in 2 or 3 woks, it's a comfort to know that dessert is made and chilling in the refrigerator. Try this after a curry dinner, too, or anytime you want a light, fresh and truly spectacular dessert.

8 servings

8 large oranges	1 cup sugar
⅔ cup water	¼ teaspoon cream of tartar
⅔ cup Marsala *or* orange liqueur	Juice of 1 lemon

Remove zest from all oranges with zester, small sharp knife or vegetable peeler, taking care not to include bitter white pith. Cut into thin julienne strips. Set zest and whole oranges aside.

Combine remaining ingredients in a heavy saucepan. Bring slowly to a boil, stirring occasionally. Add orange strips and simmer until syrup is reduced by approximately ⅓. Cool.

With small sharp knife, remove all remaining peel and pith from oranges. Holding oranges over plate or bowl to catch juices, cut crosswise into thin slices. Put each orange back together again by placing a long wooden pick through center to hold slices in their original alignment. Add juice to syrup.

Arrange oranges in bowl (preferably glass). Spoon syrup over all, decorating each orange with some of the caramelized peel. Chill.

Strawberries in Fondant Chemises

If the weather is cool, berries can be dipped in advance and taken to a weekend retreat in empty egg cartons.

6 servings

2 3-ounce packages cream cheese, room temperature	2 tablespoons kirsch
	Whipping cream (optional)
3 cups powdered sugar	4 cups large strawberries,
2 egg yolks	preferably with stems

Beat cream cheese until light and fluffy. Add sugar, yolks and kirsch and continue beating until fondant has reached dipping consistency. Add cream if mixture seems too thick, blending well. Dip each berry halfway in fondant and place on baking sheet or waxed paper in cool area until firm.

❦ *Swiss Meringue Techniques and Basic Recipes*

Swiss Meringue, also known as hard meringue, may be used to create spectacular edible serving containers for fresh fruit desserts. It requires more sugar and consequently more beating than does the more familiar soft meringue used for pie toppings, and is baked—basically dried—at a low temperature for an extended period of time to achieve its crisp texture.

Great Hints
- To keep Swiss Meringue from darkening during baking, use solid vegetable shortening for greasing the baking sheet—it can withstand a lengthy baking period without discoloring.
- Separate eggs directly from the refrigerator; they will break cleanly and the yolk of a cold egg is less likely to shatter than a yolk at room temperature.
- It is critical that no egg yolk find its way into the whites, as even a trace of yolk will prevent beaten whites from reaching full volume.
- Egg whites that have been refrigerated for up to 2 weeks produce a better meringue than do fresh ones.
- The acidic properties of cream of tartar stabilize the meringue, and salt helps solidify the protein in the egg whites.
- You can make your own superfine sugar by whirling granulated sugar in the blender or processor.

Swiss Meringue

Makes about 3 cups

4 egg whites, room temperature	1 cup superfine sugar
¼ teaspoon salt	½ teaspoon vanilla
¼ teaspoon cream of tartar	

Oranges with Cranberry Coulis

A light and refreshing fall treat.

10 servings

Cranberry Coulis
- 3 cups fresh cranberries, rinsed and sorted
- 1½ cups sugar
- 6 tablespoons Grand Marnier
- 2 cups water

- 6 large navel oranges
- 3⅓ cups sugar
- 1 cup water

Fresh mint leaves (garnish)

For coulis: Chop cranberries in processor using on/off turns or by hand. In blender or processor blend in 1½ cups sugar and Grand Marnier until smooth. Strain through fine sieve into bowl. Add 2 cups water. (*Coulis can be prepared up to 2 weeks ahead.*)

Remove peel from 2 oranges using vegetable peeler. Reserve oranges. Cut peel into julienne.

Beat egg whites in large mixing bowl at low speed until foamy. Add salt and cream of tartar. Gradually increase mixer speed to moderately high until egg whites form soft peaks (when beaters are withdrawn, tips of peaks will be floppy). Beat in sugar 1 tablespoon at a time, beating well after each addition.

Beat in vanilla, increase mixer speed to high and beat until sugar has completely dissolved and the mixture holds stiff peaks when beaters are removed. To test for stiffness, draw the flat side of a spatula through whites, scraping bottom of bowl; path of the spatula should stand upright without sagging.

To bake: Grease baking sheet with vegetable shortening and generously dust with flour, shaking off the excess flour, or line lightly greased baking sheet with parchment paper.

For meringue ovals: Preheat oven to between 200°F and 225°F. Using 2 spoons, shape meringue into mounds of desired size and drop onto prepared sheet. Or use pastry bag fitted with #5, #6 or #7 star tip to pipe out rosettes or ladyfingers. Bake 40 to 60 minutes. Allow to dry in oven, with door closed, for 1 hour. Cool on racks.

For layers: Preheat oven to 200°F. Press the rim of 8- or 9-inch cake pan or 2-inch cookie cutter into flour on baking sheet to make guide, or trace around edges of pan or cookie cutter on parchment paper with a pencil. Spread meringue ¼-inch thick within edges of circles or use pastry bag fitted with #5 plain tip to pipe meringue spiral, starting in center of circle, and fill in completely. Bake until thoroughly dry, 1 to 2 hours for large layers or 30 to 60 minutes for small rounds. Allow to dry in oven, with door closed, for 1 hour. Remove and cool on racks.

Cut two 12-inch-long sheets of parchment paper. Brush 1 with vegetable oil. Sprinkle other with ⅓ cup sugar. Heat remaining 3 cups sugar with 1 cup water in heavy large saucepan over low heat until sugar dissolves, swirling pan occasionally. Increase heat to medium and bring to boil. Add orange peel and boil until tender, about 10 minutes. Remove peel from syrup using slotted spoon and place on oiled paper, separating strands with fork. Continue boiling syrup until it registers 228°F on candy thermometer. Stir orange peel back into syrup and remove immediately using slotted spoon. Set on sugar-sprinkled paper. Roll peel in sugar to coat, then separate strands using 2 forks. Let cool. *(Can be stored 2 weeks in airtight container.)*

Peel remaining 4 oranges. Cut white pith off all 6 oranges. Slice oranges into thin rounds. Cover and chill.

Just before serving, spoon 3 tablespoons coulis onto each of 10 dessert plates. Place orange slices atop coulis. Sprinkle with candied orange peel and garnish with mint.

Amaretto Oranges with Sorbet

If sorbet is not available, sherbet may be substituted.

6 to 8 servings

4 to 5 large navel oranges, peeled and thinly sliced into rounds
¼ cup amaretto
1 to 1½ pints lemon *or* grapefruit *or* melon sorbet

Fresh mint leaves *or* scented geranium leaves (optional garnish)

Place orange slices in bowl and sprinkle with liqueur. Refrigerate until serving time. Drain slices and arrange in overlapping fan pattern on dessert plates. Using 2 tablespoons, scoop sorbet into 6 to 8 egg-shaped mounds and set each on plate at base of fan pattern. Garnish with leaves and serve immediately.

Orange Catalonian Cream

12 servings

6 cups milk
2 2½-inch cinnamon sticks
1 vanilla bean, split lengthwise
Grated peel of 2 large oranges
⅛ teaspoon salt
¼ cup cornstarch

¼ cup cold milk
8 egg yolks, room temperature
2 cups superfine sugar

12 teaspoons superfine sugar (garnish)

Combine milk, cinnamon sticks, vanilla bean, orange peel and salt in heavy large saucepan and bring to simmer over medium-high heat. Reduce heat and simmer gently 5 to 6 minutes. Meanwhile, whisk cornstarch and cold milk in small bowl until smooth. Whisk yolks with 2 cups sugar in large bowl until light and creamy. Blend cornstarch mixture into yolks. Remove cinnamon sticks and vanilla bean or strain milk into another large saucepan if smooth-textured custard is desired. Stir about ½ cup hot milk into yolk mixture and blend well. Gradually whisk yolk mixture back into hot milk. Place over medium heat and cook until mixture thickens and almost boils, about 10 minutes. Divide orange cream among 12 ovenproof ½-cup custard cups. Let cool.

Preheat broiler. Sprinkle 1 teaspoon superfine sugar over top of each cup of orange cream. Set cups in roasting pan lined with ice. Broil until sugar topping is rich golden brown. Cool, then refrigerate until ready to serve.

Flan de Naranja

Make sure you have 1 of the following at hand: six 1-cup custard cups, a 6-cup flan pan, heatproof baking dish or mold, or a 1½-quart soufflé dish.

6 servings

½ cup sugar
2 tablespoons water

1 orange

1 cup milk
1 cup whipping cream

1 cinnamon stick
½ teaspoon vanilla

3 eggs
1 egg yolk
¾ cup sugar

Bring ½ cup sugar and 2 tablespoons water to boil in heavy-bottomed small pan over high heat. Reduce heat and continue cooking without stirring until syrup turns deep golden brown.

If using individual custard cups, carefully divide caramel among them and swirl syrup to coat bottom and part of sides. If using large dish or mold, pour all of caramel in bottom and tip until evenly covered.

Preheat oven to 325°F. Remove outer peel of orange and set aside. Remove white pith and outside membrane; discard. Separate orange sections carefully. Set sections aside.

Combine peel, milk, cream and cinnamon stick and bring almost to boil over moderate heat. Remove pan from heat. Discard orange peel and cinnamon stick. Stir in vanilla.

Beat eggs and yolk. Add sugar slowly, beating continuously, until mixture is pale yellow and thick. While still beating, slowly pour in milk mixture. Strain through sieve.

Arrange orange sections in bottom of flan pan or dish, pressing firmly into caramel (or use 2 orange sections in each individual cup). Carefully pour in enough custard mixture to reach almost to top. Place in shallow pan partially filled with boiling water. Bake until knife comes clean when inserted into center of custard, individuals 40 to 45 minutes, flan 45 to 50, and soufflé about 55 minutes. *Lower heat if water begins to simmer.* Cover and refrigerate at least 6 hours.

Unmold custard by running sharp knife around edge and dipping bottom into hot water very briefly. Place chilled plate on top and invert, tapping on bottom to slide custard out. Spoon any extra caramel sauce over top.

Orange Flan

A not-so-traditional version of caramel custard, made with lemon and orange juices instead of whipping cream.

8 servings

⅔ cup sugar
3 tablespoons water

1 cup minus 2 tablespoons sugar
Peel of 1 orange, minced
Peel of 1 lemon, minced
2 tablespoons (¼ stick) unsalted butter, room temperature

8 eggs, separated
5 tablespoons all purpose flour
1½ cups fresh orange juice
¼ cup fresh lemon juice

Position rack in center of oven and preheat to 350°F. Fill roasting pan half full with hot water and set in oven.

Combine ⅔ cup sugar with water in heavy 1-quart saucepan and bring to boil, tilting and tipping pan until sugar is completely dissolved. Continue boiling, swirling pan frequently, until liquid is caramel in color. Working quickly, pour syrup into 1½-quart ring mold, tipping mold so inside is completely coated with caramel. Set aside.

Combine remaining sugar and citrus peels in processor work bowl or other large bowl. Add butter and blend in processor or with electric mixer. Add egg yolks and flour and mix until smooth. Add juices and blend well.

Using electric mixer, beat egg whites in separate bowl until stiff but not dry. Mix ¼ of whites into custard mixture, blending thoroughly by hand. Fold in remaining whites. Pour into caramelized mold.

Set mold in water bath and bake 40 minutes. Remove from water bath and let stand at room temperature 1 hour. Refrigerate at least 3 hours or overnight. To serve, run spatula or flexible knife around edge of custard to loosen and invert onto plate.

Papaya with Raspberry-Lime Sauce

Raspberry-Lime Sauce can be prepared up to 2 days ahead and refrigerated. Bring to room temperature before serving.

6 servings

2 10-ounce packages frozen sweetened raspberries, thawed
2 tablespoons fresh lime juice

2 tablespoons sugar
3 papayas, halved and seeded

Combine raspberries, lime juice and sugar in processor or blender and puree until sugar is dissolved and mixture is smooth. Strain to remove seeds. Place papaya halves on individual dessert plates. Spoon raspberry sauce into papaya cavities and serve immediately.

Sliced Fresh Peaches with Vanilla

Dessert may be prepared 1 day ahead.

16 to 18 servings

10 large ripe peaches
   Boiling water
1 teaspoon vanilla

⅓ cup fresh lemon juice
   Sugar
   Pinch of cinnamon

Place peaches in large bowl and just cover with boiling water. Let stand 1 minute. Drain; rinse with cold water. Peel; cut each peach into 10 slices. Mix with vanilla, lemon juice, sugar to taste and cinnamon. Chill. Drain before serving.

Peach Fantasy

10 to 12 servings

Filling
   5 tablespoons cornstarch
   ¼ cup dry Sherry
   2 tablespoons fresh lemon juice

   6 large fresh peaches, peeled and sliced*
   ¼ cup sugar
   ½ teaspoon cinnamon
   ¼ teaspoon almond extract
      Dash of nutmeg
   ½ teaspoon grated lemon peel

Meringue
   8 large egg whites

   ½ teaspoon cream of tartar
   2 cups sugar

Chocolate
   1 cup (6 ounces) chocolate chips
   ¼ cup (½ stick) butter
   ¼ cup vegetable shortening

   6 to 12 fresh peach slices, dipped in fresh lemon juice

   3 cups whipping cream

For filling: Place cornstarch in small bowl. Add Sherry and lemon juice and stir until cornstarch is dissolved.

Place peaches in blender or processor and puree. Pour into medium saucepan and blend in sugar, cinnamon, almond extract and nutmeg. Stir in cornstarch mixture. Cook over medium heat, stirring constantly until thickened and clear, about 5 minutes. Remove peaches from heat and add lemon peel. Cool, then refrigerate overnight.

For meringue: Cut out 6 waxed paper circles 8 inches in diameter. Invert six 8- to 9-inch round cake pans and grease. Place circle on each pan and grease.

Arrange oven racks in upper and lower thirds of oven. Preheat oven to 250°F. In large mixing bowl, beat egg whites and cream of tartar until foamy. Gradually add sugar, a tablespoon at a time, and continue beating until stiff and glossy but not dry.

Carefully spread meringue over waxed paper circles, smoothing with spatula. Place pans evenly in oven, 3 pans per rack, and bake until meringues are firm but

ringues dry with oven door

days in advance and stored

and shortening in top of

requently until chocolate is

chocolate and place on

eringue plain. Allow choc-

hocolate-topped meringue

Continue with remaining

e. Spread with remaining

es of dessert. Place remain-

pipe rosettes around sides

es. Refrigerate 2 to 4 hours

ay be substituted for fresh.

ons apricot brandy

l)

pping cream

ons superfine sugar

n vanilla

aucepan and bring to boil

er 10 minutes. Transfer to

aucepan.

d potato starch to pureed

at 5 minutes, stirring fre-

d in brandy. Spoon into 6

rving, whip cream, adding

ench vanilla ice cream,

softened

dd peaches and mix thor-

spberry mixture over top,

CW

PERSONNEL
SERVICES

1050 SEVENTEENTH STREET, N.W. • SUITE 270 • WASHINGTON, D.C. 20036
202-296-7530

[handwritten notes]

Flour tortilla

tea

Fantasy Ranch

Deep dish chili cheese Pie

7 mild dry green chiles

15 oz garbanzo Beans

frozen corn

1 LB shop cheese

2/3 cup yellow cornmeal

Chives

flauta tart   shredd BQ

1 pd lean Beef -

green chiles

12" flour tortill - 1/2 cup monton

sour cream   Jack

avocado   cheese

❦ Speedy Summer Peach Desserts

- Toss sliced fresh peaches with 2 tablespoons fresh lemon juice, then fold into sour cream. Flavor with orange liqueur. Serve on thin slices of pound cake.
- Cover and bake peeled peaches in a syrup of 1 cup port wine, 1 cup sugar, juice of 1 lemon and ½ teaspoon cinnamon in a 350°F oven 45 minutes. Serve chilled, topped with crème fraîche or sour cream.
- Beat 1 quart vanilla ice cream to soften, then mix in ¼ cup anise liqueur. Serve over fresh poached peaches and garnish lightly with chocolate curls.
- Place peeled, sliced fresh peaches in baking dish. Spread with layer of sour cream. Cover completely with light brown sugar and broil just until sugar is caramelized.
- Marinate 6 peeled, halved and pitted peaches in 2 tablespoons orange liqueur and ¼ cup honey. Refrigerate. When ready to serve, place 2 peach halves in each of 6 large wine glasses and add Champagne to cover. Garnish each portion with 1 perfect long-stemmed strawberry.
- To make peach butter, put ½ cup peeled, sliced peaches, 1 cup (2 sticks) unsalted butter and ½ cup powdered sugar in blender or processor. Whirl until smooth. Chill and spread on crepes, then fill with fresh peaches and heat. (This butter is also delicious on toast or with muffins, waffles or pancakes.)

Amaretto Peaches Filled with Amaretto Zabaglione

For variation, serve zabaglione in baked tart shells. Top with sliced peaches.

8 servings

4 egg yolks, room temperature
1 tablespoon sugar
½ cup amaretto
½ cup whipping cream
⅓ cup fresh orange juice

¼ cup amaretto
8 medium-size ripe fresh peaches, peeled
3 tablespoons coarsely ground unsalted pistachio nuts

Combine yolks and sugar in top of double boiler set over simmering water. Whisk in ½ cup liqueur, whisking constantly until mixture is thick; *do not boil.* Transfer mixture to medium bowl, stirring several minutes to cool. Refrigerate until mixture is well chilled.

Beat whipping cream in medium bowl until stiff peaks form; fold gently into egg mixture. Chill zabaglione 1 hour.

Combine orange juice and ¼ cup liqueur in small bowl and set aside.

Slice small piece from bottom of peach and stand fruit upright. Trim ½ inch from opposite end. Using small sharp knife, cut around pit, leaving ½-inch shell. Hollow out center with teaspoon. Repeat with remaining peaches. Sprinkle fruit generously with orange juice–liqueur mixture. Chill.

Shortly before serving, drain peaches well. Pat centers dry with paper towel. Fill with zabaglione, mounding slightly. Sprinkle with pistachio nuts and serve. (Color of zabaglione may vary according to intensity of egg yolks.)

Baked Pears in Cider Syrup

6 servings

6 firm ripe pears (unblemished)
1 small lemon, halved
2½ cups unsweetened apple cider
½ cup sugar
Continuous strip of peel from 1 small lemon

1 vanilla bean, split lengthwise
1 small cinnamon stick

1½ cups whipping cream (optional garnish)
1½ tablespoons brandy (optional)

Peel pears with vegetable peeler, leaving stem intact and rubbing exposed parts with cut side of lemon as you work to prevent discoloration. Trim bases of pears slightly if necessary so fruit stands upright. Combine cider, sugar, lemon peel, vanilla bean and cinnamon stick in nonaluminum large saucepan and bring to boil over medium-high heat. Add pears in single layer, spacing evenly. Reduce heat to low and simmer gently until just fork tender, about 30 minutes. Let pears cool in liquid, partially covered.

Whip cream in large bowl of mixer to soft peaks. Blend in brandy. Transfer pears to serving dish. Reduce liquid remaining in pan to syrupy consistency. Pour syrup over pears. Serve immediately or cool to room temperature. Serve whipped cream separately.

Braised Pears à la Bressane

6 servings

6 firm ripe pears, peeled, cored and halved
¼ cup sugar
3 tablespoons unsalted butter, cut into bits

2 cups whipping cream, room temperature

3 to 4 tablespoons Cognac
2 to 3 tablespoons honey
½ teaspoon vanilla

Preheat oven to 400°F. Place pears, cut side down, in single layer in 9 × 13-inch baking dish. Sprinkle with sugar and dot with butter. Bake until tender, about 35 to 40 minutes.

Remove from oven and reduce heat to 350°F. Pour 1 cup whipping cream over pears and return to oven until sauce is thick and caramel colored, about 10 minutes, basting pears a few times with cream. Allow to cool.

Whip remaining cream with Cognac, honey and vanilla. Serve pears at room temperature. Top each serving with a dollop of whipped cream.

Fresh Peach and Blueberry Compote

8 servings

1 tablespoon frozen orange juice concentrate
1 tablespoon sugar
2 teaspoons fresh lemon juice
2 teaspoons kirsch

Grated peel of ½ orange
8 firm, ripe peaches (2½ pounds total), halved, pitted and thinly sliced
1 cup fresh blueberries

Combine first 5 ingredients in 2-quart serving bowl and blend well. Add sliced peaches to orange juice mixture. Gently blend in blueberries, tossing lightly. Cover and refrigerate at least 2 hours.

Fresh Peach Clafouti

2 servings

2 teaspoons sugar
1½ cups peeled peach slices
⅓ cup milk
⅓ cup half and half
1 egg, room temperature
2 tablespoons all purpose flour
1 tablespoon sugar

½ teaspoon vanilla
¼ teaspoon freshly grated nutmeg
Pinch of salt

Powdered sugar
Vanilla ice cream *or* whipped cream (optional)

Preheat oven to 375°F. Butter two 8-ounce au gratin dishes or 1 small baking dish. Sprinkle with 2 teaspoons sugar. Arrange peaches in single layer in dish(es). Mix milk, half and half, egg, flour, sugar, vanilla, nutmeg and salt until smooth. Pour batter over peaches. Bake clafouti until puffed and golden, 35 to 40 minutes.

Just before serving, sprinkle with powdered sugar. Serve with ice cream or whipped cream if desired.

Raspberry Poached Pears

8 servings

2 10-ounce packages frozen raspberries, thawed and undrained
½ cup crème de cassis

8 firm ripe pears

¼ cup finely chopped raw pistachios

Puree raspberries until smooth in processor or blender. Strain through fine sieve to remove seeds. Add crème de cassis to puree. *(Can be prepared ahead.)*

Peel pears. Core from bottom, leaving stem intact. Cut thin slice from bottom so pears stand upright. Arrange pears upright in large saucepan. Pour raspberry mixture over. Bring to simmer, then cover and simmer gently until tender, about 8 to 10 minutes. Remove pears from pan. Cool, then chill.

Transfer cooking liquid to smaller saucepan and boil until reduced to thick syrup, about 10 to 12 minutes. Let cool. *(Can be prepared ahead.)*

To serve, spoon some of syrup onto individual plates. Top with pears. Drizzle additional syrup over. Sprinkle pears with chopped pistachios.

Baked Pears with Caprino

6 servings

3 large pears, slightly underripe
Fresh lemon juice
3 tablespoons Port
3 tablespoons amaretto
¼ cup sugar
½ teaspoon cinnamon, or to taste
½ teaspoon mace, or to taste
¼ teaspoon ground cloves, or to taste

1 teaspoon grated orange peel *or* lemon peel, or to taste

½ pound caprino cheese
1 cup amaretti (Italian macaroon) crumbs
Fresh strawberries (garnish)

Preheat oven to 350°F. Butter 1½-quart baking dish. Peel pears, rubbing with lemon juice to prevent discoloration. Carefully remove cores through bottom. Cut thin slice from bottoms so pears stand upright. Stand pears in prepared dish. Add Port and amaretto. Mix sugar with spices to taste. Sprinkle over pears. Cover and bake 30 minutes, basting frequently.

Remove cover and continue baking, basting frequently, until pears are easily pierced with knife, 30 to 45 minutes (time will vary depending on size and ripeness of pears). Remove from liquid and cool slightly. Increase oven temperature to 375°F. Transfer poaching liquid to small saucepan. Add grated orange peel to taste. Cook over medium heat until reduced by half. Strain sauce into small serving bowl.

Slice cheese into 12 rounds. Brush lightly with pear sauce. Roll in amaretti crumbs. Set on baking sheet. Bake until heated through, 5 to 10 minutes. Cut pears in lengthwise slices and arrange on plates. Top with fresh strawberry. Accompany with warmed cheese. Serve sauce separately.

Almond Poached Pears

2 servings

¾ ounce slivered almonds

2 medium pears

1 egg yolk
¼ cup powdered sugar
⅛ teaspoon almond extract

½ cup dry white wine
2 tablespoons amaretto

¼ cup whipping cream
2 teaspoons powdered sugar
⅛ teaspoon almond extract

Position rack in center of oven and preheat to 375°F. Spread almonds in baking dish and toast in oven 6 to 8 minutes, stirring occasionally. Let cool, then chop finely. Set aside 2 teaspoons chopped almonds for garnish. Retain oven temperature at 375°F.

Peel pears. Cut off stem ends. Cut thin slice from bottoms so pears stand upright. Using thin-bladed knife or coring tool and long-handled small spoon, core pears from stem end and scoop out about half of pulp from inside, leaving bottom and sides intact.

Beat egg yolk until light and lemon colored. Add ¼ cup powdered sugar and continue beating until thick and fluffy. Stir in ⅛ teaspoon almond extract and all almonds except garnish. Fill pears evenly with mixture. Stand pears upright in nonaluminum baking pan just large enough to accommodate them. Pour wine and liqueur into pan. Cover and bake 30 minutes. Baste outside of pears with cooking liquid (being careful not to drip liquid into centers) and continue baking 10 more minutes, basting again after 5 minutes. Transfer pears to serving dishes. Place baking pan over medium-high heat and boil cooking liquid until reduced to 2 tablespoons. Spoon over pears.

Whip cream in small bowl until stiff peaks form. Fold in 2 teaspoons powdered sugar and ⅛ teaspoon almond extract. Top pears with cream. Sprinkle with reserved almonds and serve.

Sparkling Raspberries

4 servings

2 cups (1 pint) fresh raspberries, rinsed and drained

1 bottle sparkling Muscat

Place raspberries in serving dishes. Pour about 1 generous tablespoon wine over each serving. Serve immediately accompanied by glass of wine.

❦ Perfect Custard Sauces

Custard sauce or "crème anglaise," the most useful of the French dessert sauces, makes a wonderful complement to fruit desserts. It is made from only four ingredients—milk, egg yolks, sugar and flavoring.

Custard sauce is quick to prepare but requires close attention. The sauce thickens only slightly, from the gradual heating of the egg yolks. If exposed to too high heat, cooked too long or not stirred continuously, the yolks will coagulate like scrambled eggs.

Tips and Techniques

Custard Sauce

- Organization is very important. Ready all utensils—whisk, wooden spoon, strainer and mixing bowl—before beginning the recipe.
- Split vanilla bean near one end and continue almost to the other, so ends are still joined (bean can be rinsed, dried and reused several times). One teaspoon of pure vanilla extract can be substituted for the bean; add the extract to the finished cooled sauce.
- To make stirring easier and to help prevent mixture from sticking to sides of pan, use a heavy-bottomed enameled or stainless steel saucepan with a rounded rather than straight bottom.
- Be sure to reach entire bottom surface of saucepan when stirring.
- If sauce curdles and looks lumpy, gradually pour it into a blender or processor with the machine running. This will save the sauce (unless it is very badly curdled), but will make the texture frothy rather than velvety. To remedy this, let sauce stand in bowl 1 hour, stirring a few times.

Basic Custard Sauce

This recipe can be halved; custard sauce will then take approximately 7 minutes to thicken instead of 10. Finished sauce can be kept warm for up to 1 hour in top of double boiler set over hot water and stirred occasionally. Or cover sauce and refrigerate up to 2 days.

Makes 2¼ cups

2 cups milk	6 egg yolks, room temperature
1 vanilla bean, split lengthwise almost in half	5 tablespoons sugar

Combine milk and vanilla bean in heavy-bottomed medium saucepan and bring just to boil over medium heat. Remove mixture from heat and let steep for 10 to 15 minutes.

Beat yolks to blend in large bowl of electric mixer. Gradually add sugar, beating until mixture is pale yellow and forms a ribbon when beaters are lifted from bowl.

Reheat milk just to simmer. Gradually pour hot milk into yolk mixture in very thin stream, whisking constantly; leave vanilla bean in pan. Pour mixture back into pan and whisk again. Place over low heat and cook, stirring constantly over entire bottom of pan with wooden spoon, until candy thermometer registers 170°F, sauce is thick enough to coat back of spoon and finger leaves path on spoon when drawn across, about 10 minutes; *do not boil or custard sauce will curdle.*

Immediately pour sauce into bowl. Remove vanilla bean. Stir sauce to cool, about 30 seconds. Serve hot or chilled. If serving cold, cool to room temperature, stirring occasionally, or place plastic wrap on surface to prevent skin from forming.

Variations

Custard Sauce

- *Coffee Custard Sauce.* Dissolve 1½ to 2 tablespoons instant coffee powder in 2 tablespoons very hot water. Stir mixture into the finished sauce.
- *Chocolate Custard Sauce.* Omit vanilla bean. Melt 8 ounces chopped semisweet chocolate in medium saucepan set over pan of hot water over low heat. Gradually stir finished sauce into melted chocolate. Serve hot.
- *Lemon Custard Sauce.* Substitute peel, cut julienne, of 1 medium lemon (colored part only) for vanilla bean. Strain peel from sauce before serving.
- *Orange Custard Sauce.* Substitute strips of peel of 2 medium oranges (colored part only) for vanilla bean. Strain sauce before serving. For stronger orange flavor, stir 2 teaspoons (or to taste) unsweetened orange juice concentrate into finished sauce.
- *Liqueur Custard Sauce.* Omit vanilla bean if desired. Stir about 4 teaspoons Grand Marnier, kirsch or other liqueur into sauce just before serving.

Basic Glaze

8 to 10 servings

2 cups granulated sugar
⅔ cup water

Pinch cream of tartar
2 cups fresh fruits and berries

In top of double boiler, heat ingredients together to crackling stage (290° to 300°F on candy thermometer). Place top of double boiler over hot, not boiling, water. Dip thoroughly dried berries and fruits in syrup, holding by stems or using bamboo skewers. Invert fruits on waxed paper or oiled baking sheet to dry.

Ricotta and Strawberry Dessert

4 servings

1 pound whole milk ricotta cheese, room temperature
3 tablespoons sugar
½ teaspoon vanilla

2 cups (1 pint) fresh strawberries, hulled and halved
¼ cup unsalted slivered almonds, toasted

Combine cheese, sugar and vanilla and blend well. Spoon into 4 dessert dishes. Top with strawberries and almonds.

Frosted Fruits

Follow the same procedure to frost strawberries, cherries and other small whole fresh fruits.

6 to 8 servings

1 egg white
2 tablespoons water
1 cup granulated sugar

2 pounds grapes in small bunches

Lightly beat egg white with water in bowl and set aside. Pour sugar into second, shallow, bowl.

Wash and dry grape clusters. Dip each cluster into egg white, covering all surfaces and letting excess drain into bowl. Set aside on waxed paper until all grapes are dipped. Surfaces will be tacky to the touch.

Coat clusters with granulated sugar, shaking off excess. Place clusters on waxed paper to dry.

Pears and Plums in Wine

8 servings

2 oranges
¼ cup orange liqueur

8 firm ripe pears
Acidulated water (water with small amount of lemon juice added)
3 cups Bordeaux *or* other dry red wine

1½ cups sugar
1 3-inch piece cinnamon stick
1 2-inch strip lemon peel
3 whole cloves

16 red plums

½ cup currant jelly
1 tablespoon fresh lemon juice

With sharp knife, carefully remove zest from orange. Cut zest into fine strips and parboil 10 minutes. Drain and place in small bowl. Add liqueur and set aside.

Carefully peel pears without removing stems and drop immediately into acidulated water. Combine wine, sugar, cinnamon, lemon peel and cloves in 2- to 2½-quart saucepan; bring to boil over high heat. As soon as sugar is dissolved, reduce heat to low and add 2 to 3 pears. Cover and poach until tender, about 20 to 30 minutes. Remove pears from liquid and place in large bowl. Repeat with remaining pears.

When pears have been cooked, add all plums to poaching liquid; cover and cook over low heat 10 minutes. Remove and add to bowl with pears.

Reduce remaining poaching liquid over medium heat until it lightly coats a spoon and becomes slightly syrupy. Add jelly and mix until completely dissolved. Stir in lemon juice. Add reserved orange peel and liqueur and pour over fruit. Chill thoroughly.

Poached Pears with Ginger Cream

20 servings

Poached Pears
1 lemon
20 firm ripe pears

4 cups sugar
4 cups water
1 cup Sauternes *or* German *or* other white dessert wine
½ cup grated *or* finely chopped fresh ginger
¼ teaspoon salt

Ginger Cream
4 cups whipping cream

1 cup sugar
4 eggs, separated
2 teaspoons ground ginger
⅛ teaspoon salt
¼ cup amaretto

Ginger Topping
2 cups poaching liquid from pears

¾ cup slivered almonds, toasted (optional garnish)

For pears: Cut lemon in half and squeeze juice into large bowl of cold water. Peel pears; remove blossom end with small melon baller, but leave core and stem intact. Immediately plunge into water to retain color.

Combine sugar, water, wine, ginger and salt in large nonaluminum Dutch oven. Cover and bring to boil, stirring several times to make sure sugar is completely dissolved. Reduce heat to low and arrange 10 pears standing upright in bottom of pan. Cover and poach gently until pears are tender, about 30 minutes. Remove with slotted spoon and transfer to dish large enough to hold all pears in single layer. Poach remaining pears and add to dish.

Strain all but 2 cups poaching syrup over pears. Combine ginger in sieve with 2 cups syrup in 1½- to 2-quart saucepan, cover and set aside for ginger topping. Let pears cool to room temperature; cover; refrigerate overnight.

For ginger cream: Combine cream with ½ cup sugar in 2-quart saucepan and heat until glossy film forms on top; *do not boil.* Let cool slightly.

Beat egg yolks with remaining ½ cup sugar, ginger and salt in large bowl until light and fluffy. Begin adding cream a few drops at a time and beat well, then gradually add remainder. Return mixture to saucepan and cook over medium heat until custard is thick enough to coat metal spoon. Remove from heat and stir in liqueur. Let cool.

Beat egg whites until stiff but not dry. Stir about ⅓ into cooled yolk mixture to lighten custard. Gently fold in remainder. Cover and chill overnight (or process in ice cream maker).

For topping: Bring reserved poaching syrup to boil over medium-high heat. Reduce heat and simmer, shaking pan occasionally, until syrup is thickened, about 30 minutes. Keep warm in double boiler until ready to serve.

To serve, place ginger cream in balloon wine goblets or glass dessert bowls. Top each serving with a pear, a drizzle of syrup and a sprinkling of slivered toasted almonds.

🍏 Fresh Fruit Bavarian Creams

Bavarian cream is a molded dessert that can be prepared in two ways. The most common version is based on custard sauce and is flavored with vanilla, chocolate, coffee, liqueur or citrus fruit. The second kind, for which a basic recipe follows, emphasizes the natural flavor of delicate fruits. It consists of sweetened fruit puree and does not contain custard sauce. In both types, gelatin binds the mixture and whipped cream adds lightness.

After the gelatin is added, the basic mixture is left to cool completely. It should be stirred often as it cools so it will not stick to the sides and bottom of the bowl, which become cold faster than the center. The mixture will thicken, and when it is cold to the touch and quite thick, but not yet set, the cream is folded in. (There are two reasons for cooling the mixture before adding the whipped cream: A hot mixture would melt the cream and cause it to lose body, and a warm mixture would be thinner than the cream and the two would separate into layers instead of forming a smooth dessert.)

Bavarian cream is most impressive when prepared in a decorative mold and turned out onto a platter. The shape of the mold determines the setting time: A mixture takes longer to set in a deep bowl, for example, than in a ring mold. Of course, these desserts can also be prepared in a deep, attractive dish and served directly from that. In this case, only two-thirds of the gelatin quantity given in the recipe is needed. Garnishes need not be elaborate—a few rosettes of whipped cream or fresh fruit slices will complete the picture.

Tips and Techniques

Bavarian Cream

- To speed the cooling process, set hot gelatin mixture in a container of ice cubes instead of in the refrigerator; stir frequently to prevent mixture from setting at sides of bowl.
- If gelatin mixture accidentally sets, the cream will form lumps when folded in. To prevent this, whisk the set mixture until smooth, then lightly stir in whipped cream using whisk.
- To facilitate adding cream, fold in half the cream to lighten mixture, then gently fold in remaining cream.
- Use plain molds or those with simple designs to prevent sticking.
- For quick setting of nonfruit bavarians, chill dessert in freezer. Thaw in refrigerator before serving.
- If some of cream sticks after turning out of mold, carefully put it in place and smooth gently with moistened spatula. Patches can be further camouflaged with garnishes of whipped cream and fresh fruit slices.
- To attain greater volume when whipping cream, chill beaters of portable electric mixer and bowl.

Bavarian Cream Pudding

For an attractive presentation, prepare this dessert in a ring mold and garnish the center of the ring with sliced fresh fruit after unmolding onto serving platter.

6 to 8 servings

2 cups thinly sliced mixed fruit (at least 2 of the following: strawberries, peeled peaches, nectarines, apricots, seedless grapes, oranges *or* tangerines)
2 tablespoons sugar
2 tablespoons kirsch
1 envelope unflavored gelatin
¼ cup water
1 cup milk

1 vanilla bean, split lengthwise almost in half
3 egg yolks
½ cup sugar

2 tablespoons kirsch

1 cup whipping cream
6 3½-inch ladyfingers, split lengthwise or halved crosswise

Gently mix fruit with 2 tablespoons each sugar and kirsch in small bowl. Cover and refrigerate 1 hour.

Sprinkle gelatin over water in small cup. Prepare Basic Custard Sauce using amounts of milk, vanilla and yolks indicated above and remaining ½ cup sugar; custard sauce will take only about 4 minutes to thicken.

As soon as sauce is thickened to correct consistency, remove vanilla bean. Immediately add gelatin and whisk until completely dissolved. Pour custard into large bowl. Cool to room temperature, stirring occasionally, about 30 minutes. Meanwhile, refrigerate another large bowl and beaters of portable electric mixer. Lightly oil 6-cup mold or bowl. Set aside.

Stir kirsch into cooled custard. Refrigerate until cold and beginning to thicken, about 15 to 20 minutes, stirring mixture every 5 minutes; *do not allow custard mixture to set.*

Using slotted spoon, transfer fruit to custard and blend gently; reserve liquid. Refrigerate custard 2 minutes to thicken slightly, stirring twice.

Whip cream in chilled bowl with chilled beaters just to soft peaks. Gently but thoroughly fold cream into custard. Refrigerate until beginning to set, about 5 minutes, folding occasionally. Spoon half of cream mixture into prepared mold. Dip 1 ladyfinger half briefly into reserved liquid and set atop cream mixture. Repeat with 5 more ladyfinger pieces, spacing evenly. Refrigerate 2 minutes. Carefully spoon remaining cream mixture over top of ladyfinger layer. Dip remaining ladyfingers into reserved liquid and set on top. Press top layer to level. Cover with plastic wrap. Chill until completely set, at least 2 hours.

To unmold and serve, dip mold for about 10 seconds into enough warm water to come nearly to top of mold; pat dry. Run thin-bladed flexible knife around edge of bavarian, gently pushing mixture slightly from edge of mold to let in air. Set platter atop mold, grip mold and platter tightly and invert bavarian and platter together. Shake mold downward once; dessert should release onto platter. If dessert remains in mold, redip in warm water several seconds or surround with towel that has been dipped in hot water and wrung dry. Carefully remove mold by lifting straight upward. Smooth top and edges with spatula. *(Do not unmold until several hours before serving; return to refrigerator. Let stand at room temperature for about 10 minutes before slicing and serving.)*

Pineapple Bavarian Cream

Finished sauce can be kept warm for up to 1 hour in top of double boiler set over hot water. Stir occasionally.

8 servings

Poaching Syrup
3½ cups water
1 cup sugar
1 tablespoon fresh lemon juice
1 medium pineapple (about 4 pounds), peeled and cut crosswise into ½-inch slices

Custard Sauce
1 cup milk

1 vanilla bean, split lengthwise almost in half

4 egg yolks, room temperature
⅓ cup sugar

1 envelope unflavored gelatin

1 cup whipping cream

For syrup: Combine water and sugar in large saucepan and bring to boil over low heat, swirling pan gently until sugar is dissolved. Stir in lemon juice. Add pineapple and bring to simmer. Reduce heat to low and poach until slices can be pierced easily with sharp knife, about 10 minutes (pierce side of fruit, not tough core). Remove from heat and let stand in syrup until cool, at least 2 hours. *(Syrup can be prepared 1 day ahead and refrigerated.)*

For custard sauce: Combine milk and vanilla bean in heavy-bottomed medium saucepan and bring just to boil over medium heat. Remove mixture from heat and let steep for 10 to 15 minutes.

Beat yolks to blend in large bowl of electric mixer. Gradually add sugar, beating until mixture is pale yellow and forms a ribbon when beaters are lifted.

Reheat milk just to simmer. Gradually pour hot milk into yolk mixture in very thin stream, whisking constantly; leave vanilla bean in pan. Pour mixture back into pan and whisk again. Place over low heat and cook, stirring constantly over entire bottom of pan with wooden spoon, until candy thermometer registers 170°F, sauce is thick enough to coat back of spoon and finger leaves path on spoon when drawn across, about 7 minutes; *do not boil or custard sauce will curdle.* Immediately pour sauce into bowl. Remove vanilla bean. Let cool until just warm, stirring occasionally.

Sprinkle gelatin over ¼ cup cooled syrup and let stand about 5 minutes to soften. Bring another ¼ cup syrup to boil in small saucepan over medium heat. Remove from heat. Add softened gelatin and whisk until completely dissolved. Gradually pour gelatin mixture into custard sauce in slow steady stream, whisking constantly. Cool to room temperature, stirring occasionally, about 15 minutes.

Meanwhile, refrigerate another large bowl and beaters of portable electric mixer. Lightly oil 5- to 6-cup mold or bowl. Drain pineapple thoroughly. Drain again on paper towels. Cut out cores using small sharp knife. Cut 7 pineapple slices into ½-inch dice; reserve remaining slices for garnish. Refrigerate all pineapple.

Refrigerate custard mixture until cold and beginning to thicken, about 20 minutes, stirring every 5 minutes; *do not allow mixture to set.* Stir in diced pineapple and refrigerate until beginning to set, stirring frequently.

Remove pineapple mixture from refrigerator. Whip cream in chilled bowl with chilled beaters just to soft peaks. Gently fold half of cream into pineapple mixture, then gently fold in remaining half, blending thoroughly. Refrigerate 15 minutes if necessary to suspend pineapple pieces in cream mixture. Pour into prepared mold, smoothing top. Cover and refrigerate until bavarian is completely set, at least 2 hours.

To unmold and serve, dip mold for about 10 seconds into enough warm water to come nearly to top of mold; pat dry. Run thin-bladed flexible knife around edge of bavarian, gently pushing mixture slightly from edge of mold to let in air. Set platter atop mold, grip mold and platter tightly and invert bavarian and platter together. Shake mold downward once; dessert should release onto platter. If dessert remains in mold, redip in warm water several seconds or surround with towel that has been dipped in hot water and wrung dry. Carefully remove mold by lifting straight upward. Smooth top and edges with spatula. Cut reserved pineapple slices in thirds. Place around base of dessert. Refrigerate until ready to serve.

Fresh Pineapple Rings with Gingered Yogurt Sauce

8 servings

2 cups plain yogurt
1 tablespoon sugar, or to taste
1 teaspoon minced crystallized ginger

16 ½-inch-thick fresh pineapple rings (about 2 pineapples)

Blend together yogurt, sugar and ginger. Arrange pineapple on individual plates. Spoon sauce over and serve.

Fresh Pineapple Surprise

6 to 8 servings

Fruit
2 large pineapples (about 3½ pounds each)
¾ cup (4 ounces) dried apricots, cut into ¼-inch julienne
2 tablespoons kirsch
2 tablespoons sugar, or to taste

Italian Meringue
¾ cup sugar

⅓ cup water
3 egg whites, room temperature
½ teaspoon vanilla

Lemon leaves (garnish)
Raspberry Sauce *or* Vanilla Cream Sauce (see following recipes)

For fruit: Split pineapples lengthwise with sharp knife, cutting through leaves. Cut around inside of each half with serrated grapefruit knife, leaving ½-inch shell. Carefully remove fruit in one piece. Set aside the two best shells with leaves attached. Remove and discard pineapple cores. Cut pineapple into strips ¾ inch wide, then cut strips into ¾-inch dice. Combine pineapple, apricots, kirsch and sugar in large bowl and toss well. Cover and refrigerate at least 24 hours.

For meringue: Combine sugar and water in small saucepan and stir over medium-high heat until sugar is just dissolved. Bring to boil. As temperature of syrup approaches 200°F on candy thermometer, beat egg whites in large bowl of electric mixer at medium speed until stiff and glossy. When sugar syrup reaches soft ball stage (235°F on candy thermometer), add syrup to egg whites in slow steady stream with mixer running. Continue beating until whites are cool and very thick, about 5 minutes. Stir in vanilla. Transfer meringue to pastry bag fitted with medium star tip. *(Meringue can be prepared up to 2 hours ahead and refrigerated, tightly sealed, in pastry bag.)*

Position rack in center of oven and preheat to 425°F. Drain fruit well and divide evenly between reserved pineapple shells, mounding compactly. Pipe meringue completely over each shell, sealing to edges. Sprinkle pineapple leaves with water and cover leaves with foil. Arrange shells on baking sheet and bake until meringue is lightly browned, about 5 minutes. Line serving platter with lemon leaves. Arrange pineapples in center; discard foil. Serve with Raspberry or Vanilla Cream Sauce.

Raspberry Sauce

Can be made 5 days ahead. Recipe can be doubled or tripled.

Makes ½ cup

1 10-ounce package frozen raspberries (preferably unsweetened), thawed and drained

3 tablespoons powdered sugar (optional)
1 tablespoon kirsch

Puree raspberries in processor or blender until smooth. Press through fine sieve set over small bowl. Add sugar (if raspberries are unsweetened) and kirsch and mix well. Serve immediately, or cover and refrigerate.

Vanilla Cream Sauce

Recipe can be doubled or tripled.

Makes 2 cups

Custard Sauce
  1 cup milk
  1 2-inch piece of vanilla bean, split
  3 egg yolks

3 tablespoons sugar

1 cup whipping cream
¼ cup sifted powdered sugar

For custard sauce: Scald milk with vanilla bean in heavy small nonaluminum saucepan over medium-high heat and set aside. Combine egg yolks and sugar in medium bowl and whisk until mixture is thick and lemon colored. Gradually whisk milk into egg mixture. Return to saucepan. Place over low heat and cook, stirring constantly, until mixture thickens and coats spoon. Set pan in bowl of ice water to cool. Strain custard into medium bowl. Cover and refrigerate until well chilled. *(Can be made 5 days ahead.)*

Whip cream in medium bowl, gradually adding powdered sugar, until stiff and glossy. Gently fold cream into cooled custard sauce. Transfer to bowl. Serve immediately, or cover and refrigerate.

Pineapple Snow Eggs (Oeufs à la Neige)

Custard and meringues can both be prepared 1 day ahead, but do not assemble until just before serving.

6 to 8 servings

1½ cups coarsely chopped fresh pineapple (reserve juice)
¼ cup golden rum

Soft Custard
  6 extra-large egg yolks
  ½ cup sugar
  ½ teaspoon salt
  2 cups half and half, scalded
  1 teaspoon vanilla

Meringue Eggs

6 extra-large egg whites
¼ teaspoon cream of tartar
¼ teaspoon salt
1 cup (16 tablespoons) superfine sugar

Caramel
¼ cup sugar
¼ cup light corn syrup

Simmer pineapple and its juice 3 minutes in small saucepan over medium-low heat. Drain thoroughly and cool. Stir in rum. Cover and refrigerate several hours or overnight.

For custard: Combine yolks, sugar and salt in 3-quart saucepan and whisk quickly until silky consistency (when whisk is lifted about 2 inches from surface, mixture should form short breaking stream, not a ribbon). *Do not overbeat.* Slowly whisk in hot half and half. Place over medium heat and stir constantly with wooden spoon until mixture coats spoon. (Run finger across cream on back of spoon; it should not run together. Candy thermometer should register between 165°F and 180°F.) Transfer to mixing bowl and stir in vanilla. Place bowl in pan of ice and beat custard until cool. Cover and refrigerate until ready to use, stirring occasionally to prevent skin from forming.

For meringue: Beat egg whites until foamy. Add cream of tartar and salt and continue beating until soft peaks form. Gradually add sugar 1 tablespoon at a time, beating until stiff peaks form.

Heat 2 inches water in 12-inch nonaluminum skillet (aluminum will turn meringues gray). Bring water to boil, then reduce heat until water is gently simmering (170°F). Using ice cream scoop, add 4 mounds of meringue to skillet, rounding tops with your finger, and poach 1½ to 2 minutes per side. Remove with slotted spoon and drain on paper towels. Repeat with remaining egg whites. Cool completely.

About 4 hours before serving, combine custard and chilled pineapple-rum mixture. Pour into clear or tinted round or oval serving dish. Arrange meringues on top of custard.

For caramel: Combine sugar and corn syrup in small saucepan and cook over medium heat until caramel colored. (If sugar crystals form on side of pan, cover and boil rapidly 2 minutes; steam will wash crystals down sides of pan.) Do not stir; gently swirl ingredients in pan to mix. Syrup should be a rich caramel color. Remove from heat just before desired color is reached, as syrup will continue to darken and thicken as it cools. Cool several minutes until thickened. Dip fork into mixture and drizzle thin threads slowly over meringues. Store in cool place until ready to serve, but do not refrigerate.

Red and Purple Plums in Spiced Wine

Plums can be prepared 1 day ahead and chilled. For variation, serve plums with a hot caramel sauce.

4 servings

1 cup Bardolino *or* Zinfandel wine
½ cup sugar
6 peppercorns
6 whole aniseed
3 whole bay leaves
1 whole clove
1 3-inch piece cinnamon stick, halved

3 firm ripe red plums, unpeeled, pitted and quartered
3 firm ripe purple plums, unpeeled, pitted and quartered

2 tablespoons (¼ stick) butter

Fresh grape leaves *or* citrus leaves (garnish)

Combine wine, sugar, peppercorns, aniseed, bay leaves, clove and cinnamon stick in nonaluminum 8-inch skillet. Place over high heat and boil until sugar is dissolved and mixture is reduced by ¼. Add plums and continue boiling over high heat until slightly softened, about 5 minutes; *do not overcook.* Remove plums from skillet using slotted spoon and set aside. Discard seasonings, reserving cooking liquid.

Boil cooking liquid until thickened and reduced, about 5 to 7 minutes. Stir in butter and boil for another 30 seconds.

Line individual serving dishes with grape or citrus leaves. Arrange plums over leaves, top with sauce and serve.

Iced Lime Dessert

4 to 6 servings

1 12-ounce package frozen raspberries, thawed
3 tablespoons cherry-flavored liqueur

Lime sherbet

Place raspberries in blender or processor and puree. Stir in liqueur and pour over scoops of sherbet.

Fresh Raspberries with Grand Marnier Sauce

8 to 10 servings

¾ cup sugar
1 teaspoon cornstarch
¾ cup water
   Finely grated peel of 1 orange
   Finely grated peel of 1 lemon
½ vanilla bean, split lengthwise
8 egg yolks, lightly beaten
1 envelope unflavored gelatin softened in 2 tablespoons cold water

2 cups whipping cream
⅓ cup Mandarine Napoléon liqueur
⅓ cup Grand Marnier
1 quart fresh raspberries

Combine sugar and cornstarch in top of double boiler and mix well. Stir in water, orange and lemon peels and vanilla bean. Set over simmering water and stir constantly until mixture begins to thicken, about 5 minutes. Stir small amount into egg yolks, then add yolks to pan and continue cooking, stirring constantly, until thickened, about 5 minutes. Stir in gelatin, blending thoroughly. Remove from heat and strain into large bowl. Cover and chill.

Whip cream until soft peaks form. Fold into chilled mixture. Add liqueurs and stir until smooth. Arrange raspberries in large glass serving bowl and pour sauce over.

Raspberries in Crepes with Pear Sorbet (Framboises en Crepes au Sorbet Poire)

Sorbet is best if served within 24 hours. Crepes can be filled with raspberries up to 4 hours before serving.

8 servings

Sorbet
⅔ cup sugar
⅔ cup water

2 29-ounce cans pear halves, drained and pureed
¼ cup fresh lemon juice
2 tablespoons pear brandy

Melted butter
8 crepes with minced zest of ½ orange added to batter
2 cups fresh raspberries
   Crème Fraîche (see following recipe)

For sorbet: Combine sugar and water in small saucepan and stir over medium-high heat until sugar is dissolved. Just before syrup reaches boiling point, remove from heat. Let cool, then cover and refrigerate until chilled.

Combine syrup, pear puree, lemon juice and brandy. Freeze in ice cream maker or in freezer. If using freezer, turn into metal pan and freeze solid.

Partially thaw sorbet, then beat in processor until smooth and fluffy. Turn into airtight plastic container and refreeze until ready to serve.

To assemble, brush butter over one side of each crepe. Place ¼ cup raspberries in center of buttered side. Fold in sides, then ends, to form an envelope. Transfer to serving plate and place scoop of sorbet alongside. Serve immediately with Crème Fraîche.

Crème Fraîche

Crème Fraîche will keep covered in refrigerator for 10 days to 2 weeks.

Makes about 1 cup

1 cup whipping cream	**Sugar *or* freshly grated nutmeg**
2 tablespoons buttermilk	**(optional)**

Combine cream and buttermilk in glass jar and whisk until well blended. Cover and let stand at room temperature in draft-free area, whisking several times, until mixture has thickened (about 24 hours). Chill thoroughly before using. Serve plain or with sugar or nutmeg.

Spiced Berry Compote

14 to 16 servings

5 cups frozen blackberries *or* boysenberries, thawed	**1 teaspoon cinnamon**
5 cups frozen blueberries, thawed	**¼ teaspoon ground cloves**
¼ cup cornstarch	**Pinch of freshly grated nutmeg**
1½ cups sugar, or to taste	**Lightly whipped cream (garnish)**

Drain berries well; reserve ½ cup juice. Dissolve cornstarch in juice. Combine berries in large saucepan. Add sugar and spices and bring to boil over medium heat. Blend in dissolved cornstarch, stirring constantly until slightly thickened. Cool to room temperature, then refrigerate. Turn into glass or crystal bowl and serve with whipped cream.

Quick Cream-filled Strawberries

A processor is suggested for whipping the cream since cream will be more stable, but an electric mixer can be used. The filled berries will hold at least a day in refrigerator, but are best served within 4 to 6 hours if a processor is not used for whipping.

8 to 10 servings

30 to 36 fresh jumbo strawberries, hulled	**¼ cup powdered sugar**
2 cups whipping cream	**Additional powdered sugar (garnish)**
3 tablespoons Sherry, Marsala, Cognac, rum, almond liqueur *or* orange liqueur	

From point end, split each strawberry into quarters, but do not cut clear through stem. Refrigerate.

Combine cream and wine in processor using Double Steel Blade. Allow machine to run without pusher until partially whipped. Add powdered sugar and complete whipping process, being careful not to overwhip.

Place cream in pastry bag fitted with ½-inch star tip. Pipe generously into each berry. Dust with powdered sugar.

Berries with Custard Parisienne

Prepare the custard the day before serving to allow adequate time for setting and the fullest mellowing of flavors.

8 servings

5 egg yolks
¾ cup sugar
1 tablespoon unflavored gelatin
1½ cups warm milk
3 tablespoons Grand Marnier
1 tablespoon vanilla

1 cup whipping cream, whipped
6 cups fresh berries

2 tablespoons kirsch
6 tablespoons currant jelly

Combine yolks and ½ cup sugar in top of double boiler and beat until mixture is pale yellow and forms a ribbon when dropped from spoon. Sprinkle gelatin over warm milk to soften. Stir into yolk mixture, blending well. Place over simmering water and cook, whisking constantly, until custard thickens and lightly coats spoon. Add liqueur and vanilla and blend well. Pour custard into mixing bowl. Cover and chill, stirring occasionally, until custard begins to thicken (mixture will mound slightly when dropped from spoon).

Gently fold in whipped cream. Spoon custard into shallow 1½- to 2-quart glass or crystal serving bowl. Top with 2 cups of the most perfect whole berries. (Custard may also be served in individual custard or pots de crème cups.)

Puree remaining berries and sugar with kirsch in processor or blender. Press through sieve to remove seeds. Melt jelly in small saucepan over low heat. Add to berry puree and blend well. Cover and chill. Spoon over berries and custard just before serving.

Strawberries Sabayon

Plump red berries filled with rich and creamy sabayon. Strawberries may be filled 8 hours before serving, and the sabayon cream can be prepared 1 day ahead. Sabayon may also be served in dessert dishes and layered with sliced strawberries or other fresh fruits.

8 to 10 servings

30 to 36 fresh jumbo strawberries, hulled

Sabayon Cream
2 egg yolks
2 tablespoons sugar
2 tablespoons Sherry, Marsala, Cognac, rum, almond *or* orange liqueur

¼ cup powdered sugar
1 cup whipping cream

Large green leaves (decoration)
Vegetable oil
Powdered sugar (garnish)

From point end, split each strawberry into quarters, but do not cut clear through stem. Refrigerate.

For sabayon cream: In top of double boiler beat egg yolks with portable electric mixer or whisk; add sugar and Sherry or other spirit. Place over simmering water and beat until mixture is thick and forms soft peaks when beater is slowly raised, about 5 minutes.

Remove from heat and immediately place top of double boiler in bowl of ice. Continue beating until mixture is cool, about 2 minutes. Leave double boiler in bowl of ice and refrigerate 30 minutes.

Meanwhile, combine ¼ cup powdered sugar and whipping cream. Refrigerate with beater blades 30 minutes. Add chilled sabayon to cream and beat until mixture is quite stiff.

Place cream in pastry bag fitted with ½-inch star tip. Pipe sabayon generously into each berry. Refrigerate.

Wash and dry leaves and lightly rub oil over them for sheen. Place crushed ice in platter with sides. Top with leaves. Dust strawberries with powdered sugar and arrange on platter.

Strawberries with Lemon Cream

6 servings

6 cups fresh strawberries, hulled
2 tablespoons sugar

4 egg yolks
⅓ cup sugar
1 cup milk, warmed

3 tablespoons fresh lemon juice
½ cup whipping cream
Fresh mint sprigs (garnish)
2 tablespoons grated lemon peel (garnish)

Combine strawberries and 2 tablespoons sugar in bowl and toss lightly.

Combine yolks and ⅓ cup sugar in top of double boiler and beat until thick and lemon colored. Blend in warm milk. Set over simmering water and cook, stirring constantly, until custard thickens and coats spoon, about 8 minutes. Transfer custard to medium bowl. Stir in lemon juice. Chill 3 hours or up to 2 days.

Just before serving, thin custard with several tablespoons of accumulated strawberry juices. Whip cream and fold into custard. Divide berries among 6 individual goblets. Spoon lemon cream over. Garnish each serving with fresh mint and lemon peel.

Strawberries Romanoff

4 to 6 servings

1½ pounds firm ripe strawberries, hulled and quartered lengthwise (reserve 4 to 6 berries with stems for garnish)
¼ cup Cointreau *or* Grand Marnier *or* Triple Sec

¼ cup sugar
Chantilly Romanoff (see following recipe)
3 tablespoons chopped pistachio nuts (garnish)

Combine berries and liqueur in large bowl and sprinkle with sugar. Mix gently with spoon. Cover with plastic wrap and refrigerate 3 to 4 hours, spooning syrup over berries once or twice.

One hour before serving, divide berries and syrup among 4 to 6 sherbet or balloon wine glasses. Refrigerate. Just before serving, spoon Chantilly Romanoff over berries and garnish with reserved strawberries. Sprinkle each serving with pistachio nuts.

Chantilly Romanoff

Makes about 2 cups

1 cup whipping cream, well chilled
2 tablespoons Cointreau *or* Grand Marnier *or* Triple Sec

½ teaspoon vanilla
½ cup sour cream, chilled

Beat cream in large mixing bowl until slightly thickened. Add liqueur and vanilla and continue beating until soft peaks form. Fold in sour cream, then beat until mixture is thick and holds its shape. Refrigerate until ready to use.

Strawberry Cassis Parfait

2 servings

10 ounces (1⅓ cups) frozen unsweetened raspberries
2 tablespoons crème de cassis
1 tablespoon sugar

1 cup fresh strawberries, hulled and sliced
1 pint vanilla ice cream, slightly softened

Combine first 3 ingredients in processor or blender and puree. Transfer to bowl. Gently stir in sliced strawberries. Layer ice cream with strawberry mixture in 2 parfait or large wine glasses.

Crepes Ambrosia with Strawberries and Ice Cream

2 servings

2 2½-inch scoops vanilla ice cream
12 fresh strawberries, hulled
½ orange, seeds removed
1 tablespoon sugar

1 to 2 tablespoons Grand Marnier

2 teaspoons crushed toasted almonds
2 6-inch dessert crepes
1 tablespoon Cognac

Using back of spoon, make indentation on top of each scoop of ice cream. Return to freezer with 2 dessert plates.

Place 8 strawberries in sauté or crepe pan. Add orange cut side down. Sprinkle berries with sugar and cook over low heat until sugar is dissolved, about 10 minutes. Squeeze orange into pan to release juice; discard orange and stir sauce until thoroughly blended.

Increase heat to high, add Grand Marnier to pan and crush berries in the liqueur. Cook, stirring constantly, until reduced and thickened. Remove from heat and keep warm.

Sprinkle chilled dessert plates with almonds. Set ice cream in center. Place 2 strawberries on either side of scoop.

Add crepe to sauce and turn quickly to coat on both sides. Lift carefully and drape over ice cream, pushing into indentation with back of spoon. Heat Cognac, ignite and add to pan; ladle sauce over crepes and serve.

Broiled Fruit on Skewers

12 servings

1 pineapple, peeled, cored and cut into 1-inch wedges
4 bananas, cut into ½-inch slices
4 oranges, peeled, sectioned and seeded

1¾ cups superfine sugar *or* granulated sugar
1 teaspoon cinnamon, or to taste
¾ cup orange liqueur

Preheat broiler. Thread fruit evenly onto twelve 10-inch bamboo or wooden skewers, alternating pineapple, banana and orange pieces. Line broiler pan with aluminum foil. Arrange skewered fruit in prepared pan. Mix sugar and cinnamon. Sprinkle over fruit. Broil as close to heat source as possible until browned, about 3 to 5 minutes, turning occasionally. Sprinkle each with 1 tablespoon liqueur and serve immediately.

🍎 *Fresh Fruit and Cheese Finishers*

A tray piled with plump grapes, pears and apples provides a delightful dessert when accompanied by 1 or 2 good cheeses. No matter what the season, there are always fresh fruits to be fashionably dressed for dessert without breaking the calorie budget. Serve tart plums and cracked walnuts with Camembert; pears with provolone; apricots with Brie; kumquats with a touch of Roquefort.

- Mix figs in yogurt with just a sprinkling of raw or brown sugar.
- Bake bananas in their skins in a preheated 350°F oven for 20 minutes. Peel them and serve hot with a squeeze of lemon.
- Marinate pineapple in kirsch and garnish with strawberries or blueberries.
- Mix together ¼ cup honey and 2 tablespoons fresh lime juice, and spoon over thin slices of pineapple.
- Bathe papaya and pineapple chunks in plum wine.
- Cut a cantaloupe in half, remove the seeds and scoop out the melon. Dice the melon and marinate in port wine for several hours. Just before serving, return the melon to the cantaloupe shell and garnish with mint.

Fresh Fruit Compote with Limed Yogurt Topping

Vary your fruit according to season with an eye toward colorful contrast. Use of the pineapple halves as a fruit bowl makes a dramatic presentation.

6 to 8 servings

Topping
  Zest of 2 limes
¼ cup sugar
2 cups plain yogurt

Fruit Compote
1 3½-pound pineapple
6 cups additional fresh fruit (such as watermelon balls, apple slices, banana slices, strawberries, blackberries, blueberries, small clusters of seedless green grapes)

2 tablespoons fresh lime juice
2 tablespoons kirsch
1 tablespoon lime-zested sugar

Lemon leaves (optional garnish)

For topping: Combine lime zest and ¼ cup sugar in work bowl of processor and mince well by letting machine run. Fold 3 tablespoons into yogurt; reserve remaining zest for use in marinade for compote. Taste topping and add more sugar if desired. Cover and refrigerate until ready to serve.

For compote: Split pineapple, including leaves, in half lengthwise. Carefully hollow out halves, cutting into bite-size segments; reserve halves. Combine pineapple in large mixing bowl with remaining fresh fruit. Mix lime juice, kirsch and 1 tablespoon lime-zested sugar and sprinkle over fruit. Let stand several hours to blend flavors.

To serve, drain fruit and mound in reserved pineapple halves. Transfer to serving platter and garnish with lemon leaves. Serve topping separately.

Spiced Tropical Fruit

This is especially attractive when served in a hollowed-out melon.

6 to 8 servings

8 cups mixed fruit (at least 4 of the following: pineapple, watermelon *or* papaya cubes, canned mandarin orange sections *or* lichees, fresh orange and grapefruit sections), well chilled

¼ teaspoon cinnamon
¼ teaspoon freshly grated nutmeg

Mix fruit and spices; drain thoroughly before serving.

Blender Fruit Dessert

Can be frozen until ready to serve.

4 servings

1 pint vanilla ice cream, softened
1 split (2 cups) chilled Champagne

½ cup fresh *or* drained canned peaches *or* seasonal fruit

Place all ingredients in blender and whirl until smooth and creamy. Pour into stemmed glasses and serve immediately.

Fruited Trifle

Make this special dessert in your microwave.

10 to 12 servings

2 cups milk
4 egg yolks
½ cup sugar
3 tablespoons cornstarch
¼ teaspoon salt
2 tablespoons (¼ stick) butter
1 teaspoon vanilla

1 16-ounce pound cake, cut into ½-inch slices
¼ to ½ cup cream Sherry *or* rum
4 cups (2 pints) strawberries, sliced

2 bananas, peeled and sliced (about 2 cups)
1 11-ounce can mandarin orange sections, drained *or* 2 cups (1 pint) blueberries
2 kiwi, peeled and sliced
1 cup whipping cream
2 tablespoons powdered sugar
Whole strawberries (garnish)
Mint sprigs (garnish)

Combine milk, yolks, sugar, cornstarch and salt in processor or blender and mix well. Pour into medium-size glass bowl. Cook in microwave on High until thick, about 6 to 7 minutes, stirring halfway through cooking time. (Can also be cooked in heavy-bottomed saucepan over medium-high heat. Stir occasionally until mixture thickens.) Whisk in butter and vanilla. Cover custard and refrigerate until cool and softly set.

Brush cake slices generously with Sherry or rum. Arrange half of slices in single layer in trifle or other deep bowl. Layer with half of strawberries, bananas, orange sections and kiwi. Spoon half of custard over. Repeat layering with remaining ingredients. Whip cream in medium bowl until soft peaks form. Add powdered sugar and continue beating until stiff. Spoon or pipe cream decoratively over top of trifle. Garnish with strawberries and mint sprigs. Chill until ready to serve.

Fruit Compote with Raspberry Puree

6 servings

1 medium pineapple, peeled, cut lengthwise into 8 pieces, cored and thickly sliced

1 large papaya, peeled, seeded, quartered lengthwise and thickly sliced

3 large kiwi fruit, peeled, halved lengthwise and thickly sliced

1 large banana, thickly sliced

2 tablespoons kirsch
  Sugar

1 10-ounce package frozen raspberries in syrup, thawed

2 teaspoons kirsch
  Lemon leaves

Combine pineapple, papaya, kiwi and banana in large bowl. Gently stir in 2 tablespoons kirsch. Add sugar to taste. Refrigerate until ready to serve.

Puree raspberries with syrup. Press through fine sieve into small bowl to remove seeds. Stir in remaining 2 teaspoons kirsch.

Transfer fruit to 14-inch serving bowl. Arrange leaves around edge. Spoon raspberry puree into small bowls and top with fruit mixture.

Dried Fruit Compote with Spiced Wine Syrup

Makes about 6 cups

12 to 16 black peppercorns

12 to 16 white peppercorns

12 allspice berries

1 3-inch strip orange peel

1 2- to 3-inch strip lemon peel

12 ounces pitted prunes (about 2 cups)

8 to 9 ounces dried apricots (about 1¾ cups)

8 ounces small dried figs (about 1⅓ cups)

1¼ cups dry Madeira *or* Sherry

½ cup water

¼ cup honey

1 cinnamon stick

Tie peppercorns, allspice and peels in small cheesecloth bag. Transfer to heavy large saucepan. Add remaining ingredients and bring to boil over medium heat, stirring occasionally. Cover, reduce heat and simmer gently until fruit is nearly tender, about 4 to 5 minutes; do not overcook. (Can be prepared up to 1 week ahead to this point. Refrigerate fruit and syrup in separate containers until 6 to 8 hours before serving time.) Transfer to serving dish; discard cheesecloth bag. Serve compote warm or at room temperature.

Winter Fruit Compote

6 servings

6 dried prunes (with pits), soaked in water until plump
6 dried apricots, halved
1 large pear, cut into 6 wedges
1 large tart green apple, cut into 12 wedges
3 tablespoons golden raisins
1 unpeeled lemon, halved lengthwise and cut into ⅛-inch-thick slices

½ vanilla bean, split lengthwise
½ small cinnamon stick (optional)
2 cups water
6 tablespoons Port *or* Sherry

2 tablespoons slivered blanched almonds, toasted (garnish)

Combine all ingredients except almonds in large saucepan and bring to simmer over high heat. Cover partially, reduce heat to low and cook until fresh fruit is very tender and dried fruit is plump (but not falling apart), 30 to 45 minutes. Remove from heat and cool to room temperature.

To serve, remove fruit from pan using slotted spoon and divide evenly among individual goblets or bowls. If more than 1½ cups liquid remains in pan, place over high heat and reduce to 1½ cups. Spoon evenly over each serving. Garnish with almonds.

Fantasy Sundae

4 servings

2 cups fresh raspberries
1 tablespoon Grand Marnier
Sugar

2 cups (1 pint) vanilla ice cream
1 cup seedless grapes

1 cup fresh pineapple chunks
1 cup pitted bing cherries
½ cup sliced strawberries
1 peach, pitted and sliced

Combine raspberries and liqueur in processor or blender and mix until smooth. Taste and add sugar as desired, mixing well. Transfer to bowl. Cover and chill until ready to use.

Scoop ice cream into bowls. Divide fruit evenly over top. Spoon raspberry sauce over fruit.

Oriental Crackling Fruit

These may be prepared at the table and fruits may be speared individually for dipping and eating.

6 servings

2 cups granulated sugar
½ cup honey
½ cup water

4 large navel oranges,* peeled and segmented

12 large strawberries,* hulled
3 firm red apples,* cored but unpeeled and cut into eighths

In saucepan, stir together sugar, honey and ½ cup water. Bring to boil and continue boiling until small amount dropped into cold water forms hard ball (300°F on candy thermometer).

Fill shallow bowl with water and ice.

Spear orange segments, strawberries and apple wedges onto bamboo skewers. Dip skewers into hot syrup, coating fruit thinly, and plunge skewered fruit into ice water. Remove quickly and place on chilled serving plate. Serve at once.

*Equivalent amounts of other fruits such as kumquats, stuffed dates or pineapple may be substituted.

Chocolate Coating

This amount will dip 26 to 30 very large strawberries ⅔ of the way up.

4 ounces semisweet chocolate
1 tablespoon vegetable oil

26 to 30 large strawberries, washed and drained

In top of double boiler over hot, simmering (not boiling) water, melt chocolate. Stir in vegetable oil until mixture is satiny and smooth. Remove from heat and dip strawberries, draining excess back into pot. Place fruits on aluminum foil and let harden.

Quick-dipping Fondant

This amount will coat at least a quart of cherries and other small fruits. Fondant may be covered, refrigerated and used later. Simply reheat and stir to dipping consistency over simmering water in the top of a double boiler.

1½ cups granulated sugar
¾ cup water
1½ tablespoons light corn syrup

6½ cups sifted powdered sugar
Food coloring (optional)

Orange *or* lemon *or* rose water flavoring (optional)

4 cups fresh cherries *or* berries, washed and drained

Combine sugar, water and syrup in saucepan and cook over medium heat until clear and syrupy, about 10 minutes. Remove from heat. Let stand until mixture registers 170°F on candy thermometer, 3 to 4 minutes.

While syrup is still hot, gradually beat in about 6¼ cups powdered sugar. Beat until smooth, shiny and lukewarm. If fondant is too thin, gradually add more powdered sugar, beating continually. If too thick, add a teaspoon of hot water. Tint and flavor as desired.

Dip fruits into fondant, holding by stems or lightly fastened with bamboo skewer. Drain excess back into pan. Cool and harden on foil or waxed paper. Keep fondant workable by restirring over simmering, not boiling, water.

Fruit Fondue with Lemon Sauce

Approximately 18 servings

¼ cup (½ stick) butter
1 cup sugar
2 tablespoons flour
1¼ cups boiling water
½ teaspoon grated lemon peel
Dash of nutmeg

1½ tablespoons fresh lemon juice

3 cups fresh fruits, cut into bite-size pieces

Blend butter, sugar and flour in saucepan. Stirring constantly, gradually add water. Mix in lemon peel and nutmeg. Bring to boil and stir constantly until sauce is thickened, about 3 minutes. Remove from heat and blend in lemon juice.

Arrange fruit on platter around bowl of sauce. Provide toothpicks for dunking.

Minted Fruit Dip

Makes 1 cup

1 8-ounce carton lime yogurt
1 tablespoon green crème de menthe

Grapefruit sections, sliced bananas, pineapple, fresh strawberries, sliced peaches, honeydew, cantaloupe *and/or* ladyfingers

Combine yogurt and crème de menthe in small bowl and mix until thoroughly blended. Serve as dip for assorted fresh fruit and/or ladyfingers.

Mosaic of Macaroon-stuffed Fruits

An easy, do-ahead dessert that adapts well to any combination of fresh fruit. After pitting, sprinkle fruit lightly with lemon juice to prevent darkening.

6 servings

6 medium almond macaroons (about 1 cup), crumbled
5 tablespoons unsalted butter, room temperature
¼ cup skinned hazelnuts, toasted
2 teaspoons amaretto *or* ¼ teaspoon almond extract
2 teaspoons sugar
½ teaspoon grated lemon peel

2 cups fresh mint leaves (optional)
2 ripe purple plums, halved and pitted

1 ripe apricot, halved and pitted
1 ripe fig, halved
1 ripe small peach, halved and pitted
1 ripe small nectarine, halved and pitted
Fresh lemon juice
8 to 10 sweet cherries with stems
2 cups Crème Fraîche (see following recipe)

Combine macaroons, butter, hazelnuts, liqueur or extract, sugar and peel in processor or blender and mix using on/off turns until well blended. Spoon into pastry bag fitted with large star tip. Pipe 12 rosettes onto plate. Cover and refrigerate until ready to serve.

Several hours before serving, arrange mint leaves in overlapping fish-scale pattern on medium-size serving platter. Pat cut fruit dry with paper towels and sprinkle generously with lemon juice. Arrange larger pieces of fruit pitted side up in center of serving platter with smaller fruit around edges. Top each half with rosette. Scatter cherries over fruit. Cover with plastic wrap and chill. Serve with Crème Fraîche.

Crème Fraîche

Makes 2 cups

2 cups whipping cream (not sterilized or ultrapasteurized)

1 tablespoon buttermilk

Combine ingredients in jar with tight-fitting lid and shake about 30 seconds. Let stand until thickened, 8 to 24 hours (depending on room temperature). Chill at least 24 hours.

2 ❦ Mousses

Thomas Alva Edison became a millionaire because he invented the light bulb. Alexander Fleming was knighted and awarded a Nobel prize for discovering penicillin. There are statues and monuments honoring Christopher Columbus on both sides of the Atlantic. But the genius who first dreamed up the most consistently popular of all classic desserts does not even rate a paragraph in the *Larousse Gastronomique*.

This is a decidedly unfair state of events. For surely nothing is so creamily satisfying, nothing is so attractively simple—and nothing is more of a godsend to the busy host and hostess—than the mousse.

The dessert mousse has not changed very much since the Middle Ages. Eggs, cream and milk alternate as the basic ingredient, with a little unflavored gelatin sometimes added for extra body. There is an infinity of flavorings, and mousses can be molded to almost any shape, from straightforward to fanciful. They are a cinch to make, and because chilling or freezing is an essential part of the preparation, mousses are always ready to serve when dessert time rolls around.

There are, of course, many mousses that are exceptionally rich. But this chapter celebrates the lighter side of the mousse. The word originally meant "froth," and the frothy delicacies here include a Breton version flavored with apples, one made with cranberries, a chocolate-orange combination, several using berries, as well as a delicious biscuit tortoni and a lighter-than-gossamer spumante cream. Or, for a truly unusual dessert, try the sweet asparagus mousse served on almond cookies, or the pretty pastel mousse made with rose hips and white wine.

Perhaps no one really invented the mousse. Perhaps it was an accident of sorts. If so, it most certainly was—as these recipes readily prove—the happiest accident in the history of culinary arts.

Apple Mousse Bretonne

6 to 8 servings

4 to 5 tart medium apples, peeled, cored and sliced
¼ cup apricot preserves
½ teaspoon cinnamon, or to taste
¼ teaspoon freshly grated lemon peel
Pinch of nutmeg, or to taste
4 egg yolks
¾ cup sugar

1 teaspoon cornstarch
1½ cups milk, warmed
1 envelope unflavored gelatin
1 teaspoon vanilla

1 cup whipping cream

Apricot Sauce (see following recipe)

Combine apples, preserves, cinnamon, lemon peel and nutmeg in large saucepan and cook over low heat, stirring frequently to prevent scorching, until apples are very soft. Transfer mixture to blender or processor and puree. Set aside.

Place yolks, sugar and cornstarch in top of double boiler and whisk until smooth. Add warm milk. Place mixture over simmering water and cook until thoroughly heated and slightly thickened, about 20 minutes, stirring frequently. Add gelatin and vanilla and whisk until gelatin dissolves, about 2 minutes. Transfer mixture to large bowl and chill until it just begins to set.

Whip cream and fold into chilled mixture. Add apple puree and whisk gently to blend. Taste and add more nutmeg and cinnamon if desired. Pour into 6-cup mold and chill.

Just before serving, unmold onto plate; spoon some Apricot Sauce around mousse and serve remaining sauce separately.

Apricot Sauce

Makes about 1 cup

1 cup apricot preserves
2 tablespoons fresh lemon juice
2 tablespoons powdered sugar

1 teaspoon grated lemon peel
⅓ cup apricot brandy

Combine preserves, lemon juice, sugar and peel in small saucepan and cook until preserves have melted and sugar is dissolved. Add apricot brandy. Strain through sieve, then chill until just before serving.

Frozen Apricot Mousse

8 to 10 servings

2 cups finely chopped dried apricots
2½ cups sugar
2 cups water

6 eggs, separated
3 tablespoons Grand Marnier

1 cup whipping cream

Lightly sweetened whipped cream flavored with Grand Marnier (optional garnish)
Candied *or* fresh violets (optional garnish)

Combine apricots, ½ cup sugar and 1½ cups water in small saucepan. Cook over low heat until fruit is very soft, about 20 minutes. Remove from heat and cool to room temperature.

Combine egg yolks with ½ cup sugar in another saucepan. Place over low heat and whisk just until creamy; *do not boil*. Cool before blending in liqueur.

Combine remaining 1½ cups sugar and ½ cup water in third saucepan and cook without stirring over medium-high heat until syrup reaches soft ball stage (235°F on candy thermometer). While syrup is cooking, beat egg whites with electric mixer until soft peaks form. With mixer set at medium speed, slowly pour hot syrup into whites in thin stream, beating until satiny, firm and cooled to near room temperature.

Whip 1 cup cream until stiff.

Prepare 1½-quart soufflé dish with lightly oiled waxed paper collar. Fold whipped cream into cooled meringue, blending gently but thoroughly. Fold in yolk mixture, then apricots. Turn into soufflé and freeze overnight. Garnish with whipped cream and violets. Serve directly from freezer.

Sweet Asparagus Mousse on Almond Cookies (Mousse d'Asperge sur Tuiles aux Amandes)

4 servings

20 to 25 medium asparagus (fresh or frozen), tender part only
3 tablespoons sugar
1 tablespoon salt

2 egg yolks
3 tablespoons sugar

¾ cup (about) whipping cream (enough for 3/2 ratio with asparagus puree)

Almond Cookies (Tuiles aux Amandes) (see following recipe)

Cook asparagus in large pan of boiling water with 3 tablespoons sugar and 1 tablespoon salt until soft. Drain thoroughly on paper towels. Transfer to processor or blender in batches and mix until pureed. Return to saucepan and cook over very low heat, stirring constantly, until excess moisture is evaporated and puree is firm, about 10 minutes. Push through medium strainer and set aside.

Combine egg yolks with remaining sugar in top of double boiler. Set over simmering water and beat vigorously until very thick. Remove from water and continue beating until mixture is cool. Add puree and mix well.

Whip cream until stiff. Fold into asparagus mixture gently but thoroughly. Cover and chill until ready to serve.

Spoon mousse into pastry bag fitted with ½-inch plain tip. Pipe in wide ribbon down center of each cookie.

Almond Cookies (Tuiles aux Amandes)

Store in airtight can in cool, dry area.

2¼ cups sliced almonds
¾ cup sugar
¼ cup all purpose flour
3 egg whites

¼ cup (½ stick) unsalted butter, melted

Combine almonds, sugar and flour in bowl and mix well. Add egg whites and butter and blend thoroughly. Cover and refrigerate at least 1 hour.

Preheat oven to 350°F. Line baking sheet with heavy duty foil; butter generously. Drop batter by level tablespoons, leaving 5 to 6 inches between each cookie; spread batter evenly with spoon or fork. Bake until cookies are deep brown around edges and firm in center, 12 to 15 minutes. Remove from oven and let stand 30 seconds. Lift carefully from sheet using spatula. Invert tuile and curl around rolling pin or wine bottle. If cookies become too firm, return briefly to oven to soften.

🍎 *Tips for Gelatin-Based Desserts*

Molded gelatin-based mousses are particularly refreshing when temperatures rise and appetites shrink. These delicate light desserts are always spectacular, whether they are molded in an imposing scalloped cylinder or in a paper cup.

Before you use it, gelatin must be softened and dissolved in liquid. These are simple procedures, involving just a few invariable principles:

Proportions. A scant tablespoon (1 envelope) of unflavored gelatin will gel 2 cups of liquid. Additional gelatin will create a rubbery texture.

To Dissolve Gelatin. If the liquid is cold, sprinkle gelatin directly over it in a measuring cup and let stand 3 minutes to soften, then stand in simmering water and stir until melted. If the liquid is hot, sprinkle gelatin over ¼ cup of cold water and let stand 3 minutes to soften, then add to the hot liquid and stir over low heat until melted and thoroughly blended. *Gelatin should never be boiled.*

To Chill. As gelatin cools, it thickens gradually, going through several stages. The length of time it takes to reach each stage varies according to refrigerator conditions and the gelatin mixture's volume, temperature and composition.

Syrupy consistency. At this point, gelatin will be the consistency of a thick syrup and can be used to glaze fruits, pies, and cream puffs.

Unbeaten egg white consistency. At this stage, gelatin will fall from a spoon in a thick, unbroken stream. Once mixture is just past this stage, texture can be varied by whipping until fluffy.

Thickened consistency. When it reaches this stage, gelatin feels tacky and drops in uneven globs from a spoon. A fingertip will leave an impression when lightly pressed into the mixture. If you are making a multiple-layered mold, this is the time to add the next layer. The previous layer has gelled enough to prevent it from bleeding into a new layer, but not so completely that the two won't adhere. For each new layer, stir gelatin over ice until it reaches the consistency of unbeaten egg white before pouring it into the mold.

Whipped cream, stiffly beaten egg whites and pieces of fruit should be stirred in at this point in order to be evenly distributed. If added earlier, whipped cream and egg whites will separate into individual layers and fruits that are lighter than the gelatin mixture will float to the top. Once the mixture has firmed beyond the thickened consistency stage, folding in additional ingredients will result in a lumpy product.

Mousse de Kiwi Le Napoleon

8 to 10 servings

3 eggs
½ cup sugar
6 tablespoons Cointreau *or* Curaçao *or* Grand Marnier

2 cups whipping cream
¼ cup sugar

3 drops vanilla
3 kiwi fruit, peeled and finely chopped or grated
1 kiwi fruit, peeled and sliced (garnish)

To Unmold. Gelatin is ready to unmold when it is completely set and does not move when the mold is tilted. It is wise to allow at least 6 hours for this process. Stirring the mixture over ice before molding will hasten the gelling.

Run a dull knife around the edge of the mold and invert it onto a chilled serving platter that has been lightly sprinkled with water. Shake gently. If the mold does not release immediately, wring a towel out in hot water and wrap it around the outside. Repeat if necessary. To center the unmolded gelatin mixture, shake the platter gently; the water droplets will act as a hydrofoil, enabling you to slide the gelatin carefully into place.

Great Hints

- Solid ingredients should be thoroughly dried before they are added to the mold or they will make the gelatin mixture watery. Molds containing fruits must be served within 2 days to prevent discoloration of the ingredients.

- After a mixture is poured into a mold, run a knife through the center and around the sides to free air bubbles and any solid ingredients that may be trapped against the walls of the mold.

- When making a layered mold, add the heaviest layer last. After unmolding, it will be on the bottom where it will provide stability, instead of sliding off, as it might do if it were on top.

- In hot weather serve gelatin on a bed of ice to help keep it firm.

- Rinsing a mold in cold water before filling or rubbing lightly with salad oil (do not use butter or shortening, as these tend to coagulate when chilled) facilitates the unmolding process.

- Never use fresh pineapple in a gelatin mold as it contains an enzyme that prevents gelling, but cooked or canned pineapple works fine.

- Since chilling subdues flavors, overseason gelatin mixtures slightly.

- For greater stability, refrigerate goblets containing gelatin desserts in a 6-pack soft drink carton.

Break eggs into medium bowl. Add ½ cup sugar and 4 tablespoons liqueur. Set bowl into larger bowl filled with hot water. Whisk mixture until thick. Remove from water and continue whisking until cooled, 3 to 5 minutes. Cool completely in refrigerator.

Whip cream in medium bowl until thickened. Add ¼ cup sugar with vanilla and continue beating until stiff. Gently fold in chopped kiwi and remaining liqueur. Swirl egg mixture carefully into cream. Spoon mousse into large cocktail glasses or tall parfait glasses. Top with sliced kiwi. Refrigerate until ready to serve.

Perla Meyers's Cranberry Mousse

6 *servings*

Peanut *or* almond oil

2½ cups (10 ounces) whole cranberries
1¼ cups sugar
⅓ cup raisins
⅓ cup fresh orange juice
1 teaspoon cinnamon
1 teaspoon finely grated orange zest
Pinch of ground ginger

4 egg yolks

1 teaspoon cornstarch
1½ cups warm milk
2 to 3 tablespoons cranberry liqueur
1 tablespoon unflavored gelatin, softened in a little cold water
1 teaspoon vanilla

2 cups whipping cream
2 tablespoons coarsely chopped cranberries

Lightly coat 6-cup ring mold with peanut or almond oil and set aside.

Combine cranberries, half of sugar, raisins, orange juice, cinnamon, zest and ginger in heavy 3-quart saucepan. Cook over medium-low heat, stirring occasionally, until mixture is thick. Transfer to processor or blender and puree.

Combine yolks, cornstarch and remaining sugar in top of double boiler and whisk until well blended. Slowly stir in warm milk, whisking constantly. Set over simmering water and whisk until mixture heavily coats spoon, about 10 minutes. Add liqueur, gelatin and vanilla and continue whisking until gelatin is dissolved, about 1 to 2 minutes. Transfer to bowl and refrigerate until it begins to set.

Meanwhile, whip 1 cup cream until stiff. When custard begins to set, fold in cranberry puree and whipped cream. Turn into prepared mold. Cover and chill until set, about 4 hours.

Just before serving, whip remaining cream until stiff. Blend in chopped cranberries. Unmold mousse onto serving plate and mound cream in center.

Lemon Melting Moments

8 *to 10 servings*

2 cups whipping cream
½ cup superfine sugar
Juice of 4 lemons

Grated zest of 2 to 4 lemons
2 tablespoons condensed milk
8 to 10 fresh strawberries (garnish)

Combine all ingredients except berries in large, well-chilled mixing bowl and beat until very thick. Divide among parfait glasses and chill until ready to serve. Top each with a strawberry before serving.

Lemon Mousse

2 *servings*

2 teaspoons unflavored gelatin
¼ cup cold water
Grated peel and juice of 1 lemon

2 eggs, separated, room temperature

½ cup sugar
⅓ cup whipping cream, whipped

Sweetened whipped cream (optional garnish)

Sprinkle gelatin over water in top of small double boiler. Let soften 5 minutes. Set pan over boiling water and stir mixture until gelatin is dissolved. Remove from heat. Stir in grated lemon peel. Cool. Set in bowl of ice and stir just until mixture begins to thicken. Remove from ice; set aside.

Beat egg whites until foamy. Gradually add all but 2 tablespoons sugar, beating constantly until stiff but not dry. Beat egg yolks in another bowl until foamy. Gradually add remaining 2 tablespoons sugar, beating constantly until thick and lemon colored. Beat in fresh lemon juice. Add gelatin mixture and continue beating until light and thick. Fold in egg whites, blending well; then fold in whipped cream.

Pour mixture into 2½-cup soufflé dish or individual serving dishes. Chill until firm, at least 3 hours. Serve with sweetened whipped cream.

Marvelous Frozen Mango Mousse

It's a good idea to freeze mango and milk at least 8 hours (preferably overnight) before preparing mousse.

6 servings

1 very ripe large mango, peeled and cut into 1-inch pieces
1½ cups skim milk

2 tablespoons sugar
Juice of 1 lime

Arrange mango pieces on baking sheet without sides touching. Pour 1¼ cups milk into shallow pan. Freeze mango and milk until solid.

Just before serving, break frozen milk into chunks. Spoon into processor. Add remaining ¼ cup milk with sugar, lime juice and mango and mix well, stopping machine as necessary to scrape down sides of bowl, until mixture resembles smooth sherbet. (Can also be whirled in blender in batches.) Spoon into goblets or bowls.

Melon Mousse

This dessert mousse can be transformed into an unusual first course. Present in peeled melon rounds and dome with sliced prosciutto.

4 servings

8 ounces cantaloupe *or* other ripe sweet melon, peeled and seeded
Juice of ½ lemon
2 teaspoons chopped fresh mint
Pinch of salt

¼ teaspoon unflavored gelatin

¾ cup whipping cream

2 cantaloupe *or* other ripe sweet melons, halved
Fresh mint sprigs (garnish)

Puree melon in processor or blender until smooth, stopping to scrape down sides of container. (You should have 1 cup of puree.) Transfer to small bowl and add lemon juice, mint and salt. Let sit at room temperature several hours. Press through fine sieve.

Transfer puree to small saucepan. Sprinkle with gelatin and let stand several minutes to soften. Stir over low heat until gelatin is dissolved. Refrigerate until cooled and just slightly thickened, about 15 minutes.

Beat cream in chilled bowl until stiff. Stir ¼ into melon puree to loosen. Gently fold in remainder. Cover and refrigerate for several hours or overnight, folding occasionally.

To serve, mound mousse in melon halves and garnish with mint.

Chocolate-Orange Mousse

6 servings

6 medium navel oranges *or* other thick-skinned oranges

6 ounces unsweetened chocolate
1 cup sugar
2 tablespoons fresh orange juice
2 tablespoons orange liqueur

2 teaspoons grated orange peel
6 egg yolks, beaten

6 egg whites, room temperature
½ cup sugar
1 cup whipping cream

With sharp knife, slice off upper ⅓ of each orange. Remove pulp from larger sections and reserve for another use.

Melt chocolate in top of double boiler over simmering, not boiling, water. Immediately stir in 1 cup sugar. Blend in orange juice, liqueur and peel. Stir in yolks and mix thoroughly. Allow mixture to cool.

In separate bowl, beat whites until soft peaks form. Gradually add remaining ½ cup sugar and beat until stiff and glossy. Gently fold into chocolate mixture. Whip cream and fold into mixture. Spoon into orange shells and chill at least 2 hours or overnight.

Carob Mousse

4 to 5 servings

6 eggs, separated
1 6-ounce package carob chips
1 to 2 tablespoons orange liqueur (optional)
Whipped cream (garnish)

Finely ground almonds *or* almond slivers (garnish)

Beat egg yolks until thick and yellow. Melt carob chips over hot water in double boiler, stirring to avoid sticking. As soon as carob is fully melted, mix with beaten yolks and stir until smooth. Add liqueur. Beat whites until very stiff and carefully fold into carob mixture. Spoon into dessert dishes and chill to set, at least 4 hours. Remove from refrigerator just before serving. Top with whipped cream and almonds.

Fresh Strawberry Mousse

For the most spectacular presentation, divide mixture between two 1-cup soufflé dishes that have been prepared with foil collars. Remove collars just before serving to show off the mousse above edges of dishes.

2 servings

¼ cup fresh orange juice
1 envelope unflavored gelatin

1 egg
1 egg yolk
3 tablespoons sugar

6 ounces (about 1 cup) fresh strawberries, hulled

1 tablespoon framboise *or* crème de cassis *or* dark rum
⅓ cup whipping cream, whipped to soft peaks
Sliced strawberries and minced unsalted pistachios (garnish)

Oil one 3-cup mold (or two 1-cup soufflé dishes fitted with foil collars). Place orange juice in cup. Sprinkle with gelatin and let stand until liquid is absorbed, about 5 minutes.

Meanwhile, combine whole egg, yolk and sugar in medium bowl of electric mixer and beat at high speed until mixture is thick and forms a ribbon when beaters are lifted, about 5 to 7 minutes. Set aside.

Combine strawberries and framboise in processor or blender and puree until smooth. Set cup with gelatin mixture in small pan of hot water and place over low heat until gelatin is completely dissolved and clear. Stir into egg mixture. Blend in pureed strawberries. Set bowl in larger bowl of ice water and stir gently with rubber spatula until mixture is almost set, about 10 minutes. Fold in whipped cream. Pour into prepared dish(es). Refrigerate until set. If using mold, invert onto platter before serving. Garnish top with berries and pistachios.

Frozen Strawberry Mousse in a Meringue Shell

8 to 10 servings

Meringue Shells
4 egg whites, room temperature
Pinch of salt
Pinch of cream of tartar
1 cup sifted powdered sugar

Strawberry Mousse
¾ cup sugar

3 egg whites, room temperature
Pinch of salt

Pinch of cream of tartar

1 cup whipping cream
2 tablespoons kirsch

1 cup strawberries, pureed and strained

1 pint strawberries
½ cup currant jelly
1 tablespoon kirsch

For meringue shells: Preheat oven to 180°F. Beat egg whites until foamy. Add salt and cream of tartar and continue beating until soft peaks form. Add ⅔ cup powdered sugar 1 tablespoon at a time and beat until stiff and shiny. Fold in remaining powdered sugar.

Butter and flour 2 heavy baking sheets. Using 8-inch plate or cake pan as guide, draw circle on each sheet. Spoon ⅞ of meringue into pastry bag fitted with plain tube. Starting in center of each circle, pipe out 2 meringue disks in tight concentric pattern so none of baking sheet is visible. Change to fluted tube, add remaining meringue and pipe decorative edge on border of 1 circle. Bake until meringues are dry and firm but not colored, about 1¾ hours.

For mousse: Place sugar in heavy small saucepan. Pour in water just to cover. Cook over low heat until sugar melts, shaking pan occasionally. Increase heat and cook mixture without stirring until sugar syrup reaches soft-ball stage (235°F on candy thermometer).

Meanwhile, beat egg whites until foamy. Add salt and cream of tartar and beat until stiff. Gradually add syrup and continue beating until mixture is cool and thick, about 25 minutes.

In chilled bowl, beat cream and kirsch until stiff. Stir ¼ into whites; fold in remainder. Cover and freeze 2 hours.

Stir in strawberry puree. Pour mixture into 8-inch round cake pan, cover tightly and freeze for at least 4 hours.

Several hours before serving, place plain meringue on serving platter. Turn mousse over meringue and unmold (if necessary, dip towel in hot water, wring out and place over bottom of pan to facilitate unmolding). Return to freezer.

Reserve 1 large strawberry; halve remaining pint of berries. Carefully overlap halves on meringue with decorative rim; place whole berry in center. Melt currant jelly in small saucepan over low heat. Increase heat, bring to boil and stir in kirsch. Paint berries with glaze. Place meringue on cooling rack set over a tray or baking sheet and refrigerate.

To serve, slide glazed meringue over frozen mousse. Let stand at room temperature 10 minutes before serving.

Frozen Raspberry Mousse

Makes 1 quart

1 10-ounce package frozen
  raspberries in syrup
1 cup whipping cream, whipped
1 cup raspberry yogurt

1 egg white, beaten stiff
¼ cup sugar
  Melba Sauce (see following
  recipe)

Place frozen raspberries in blender or processor and whirl until smooth. Add raspberry puree to whipped cream and fold in yogurt. Beat egg white until soft peaks form, slowly adding sugar while beating. Fold egg white and sugar mixture into raspberry mixture, blending well. Spoon into chilled 4-cup glass or aluminum mold, and cover with plastic wrap. Freeze until firm. Remove mold from freezer 30 minutes before serving and refrigerate. When ready to unmold, dip mold quickly into warm water, run knife around edge and invert onto serving plate. Drizzle with Melba Sauce.

Melba Sauce

1 10-ounce package frozen
  raspberries with syrup, thawed
1 12-ounce package frozen sliced
  peaches with syrup, thawed

1 tablespoon cornstarch dissolved
  in 1 tablespoon water
2 tablespoons kirsch

Puree raspberries and peaches. Combine pureed fruit with cornstarch dissolved in water and cook over medium heat, stirring constantly, until sauce is thick and clear. Strain. Stir in kirsch. Chill thoroughly. Serve over Frozen Raspberry Mousse.

Peach Rum Mousse

8 servings

2 1-pound cans water-packed
  peaches *or* 4 large fresh peaches
½ cup honey
½ teaspoon almond extract

3 tablespoons dark rum
¼ cup fresh orange juice
2 tablespoons fresh lemon juice
1½ tablespoons unflavored gelatin
1 envelope whipped topping mix
½ teaspoon vanilla

½ cup nonfat milk

4 egg whites
  Pinch of salt

  Peach slices (garnish)
  Mint leaves (garnish)

Place foil or waxed paper collar around 1½-quart soufflé dish, or serve from large bowl or individual dessert dishes.

If using canned peaches, drain. If using fresh peaches, dip into boiling water and peel. Halve and remove pits. Reserve ½ peach for garnish. Puree remaining peaches with honey and almond extract in blender or processor.

Heat rum, orange and lemon juices in small saucepan. Remove from heat and stir in gelatin. Continue stirring until gelatin is completely melted. Blend into peach puree.

Prepare topping mix according to package directions with vanilla and nonfat milk. Fold into peach mixture and chill until slightly thickened.

Sprinkle egg whites with a pinch of salt and beat until stiff. Gently fold into peach mixture.

Spoon mixture into prepared soufflé dish or other bowl or cups. Chill about 4 to 5 hours. When ready to serve, remove collar and garnish with sliced peach and mint leaves.

Vanilla White Chocolate Mousse

4 to 6 servings

1 vanilla bean
½ cup sifted powdered sugar

4 ounces white chocolate, coarsely chopped
¼ cup (½ stick) unsalted butter, cut into 8 pieces

3 eggs, separated, room temperature

1 cup whipping cream

Pinch of salt
Pinch of cream of tartar

4 ounces dark chocolate, coarsely chopped
2 tablespoons (¼ stick) unsalted butter, cut into 4 pieces
2 tablespoons shelled pistachios, blanched, husked and minced

At least 2 days ahead, combine vanilla bean and sugar in processor or blender and mix until bean is finely ground. Pass through fine sieve, reserving large pieces of vanilla for another use. Transfer vanilla sugar to airtight container and cover. Let stand until ready to use, preferably several days or longer.

Melt white chocolate in small bowl set over hot water, stirring constantly until smooth. Whisk in butter 1 piece at a time, blending well after each addition.

Beat egg yolks with vanilla sugar until mixture is thick and pale yellow and forms a ribbon when beaters are lifted. Pour into heavy saucepan or double boiler and whisk over low heat several minutes until very thick. Whisk in melted white chocolate and continue beating until completely cool.

Beat whipping cream in chilled bowl until stiff. Beat egg whites until foamy. Add salt and cream of tartar and beat until stiff but not dry. Stir ¼ of this mixture into chocolate mixture to loosen. Gently fold in remainder until almost incorporated, then fold in whipped cream. Cover and refrigerate until set, several hours or preferably overnight.

About 15 minutes before serving, spoon mousse into goblets. Melt dark chocolate and whisk in remaining 2 tablespoons butter. Carefully spoon thin layer over each mousse and sprinkle minced pistachios in center.

Rose Mousse

6 servings

½ cup fresh orange juice
½ cup firmly packed brown sugar
1 tablespoon dried rose hips (with some leaves)
1½ teaspoons sweet white wine (preferably Johannisberg Riesling)
1½ teaspoons unflavored gelatin

¼ cup orange flower water
1 teaspoon natural orange food coloring*

2 cups whipping cream

Petals and leaves from 6 roses *or* mint leaves (garnish)

Combine orange juice, brown sugar, rose hips, wine, gelatin, orange flower water and food coloring in medium saucepan and bring to slow boil over medium heat, stirring constantly until gelatin is dissolved, about 10 minutes. Strain mixture into small bowl. Set bowl in large bowl filled with ice cubes and whisk mixture frequently until cool and slightly thickened, about 3 minutes. Set mixture aside.

Whip cream in large bowl until stiff. Gently fold in orange flower water mixture. Spoon mixture into six ½-cup ramekins or soufflé dishes. Tap dishes lightly on counter to remove air bubbles. Cover mousse with plastic wrap and refrigerate overnight.

To serve, run sharp, thin knife around molds. Invert onto individual plates. Garnish with rose petals and leaves.

*Available at natural food stores.

Almond Praline Mousse with Caramel Crown

Mousse can be layered as soon as it is made and refrigerated in goblets overnight, although praline will get slightly sticky. The caramel crown is best made no more than several hours before it is served because it absorbs moisture in the refrigerator, losing its crispness. Store layered, crowned mousse out of refrigerator in cool dry area.

4 servings

Almond Praline
⅓ cup blanched almonds

⅓ cup sugar

Amaretto Mousse
6 egg yolks, room temperature
⅓ cup sifted powdered sugar
½ cup amaretto
¼ cup fresh orange juice

1 cup whipping cream

½ cup slivered almonds, well toasted

Caramel Crown
¼ cup sugar
¼ cup light corn syrup

For praline: Preheat oven to 325°F. Bake almonds until brown, turning occasionally, about 20 minutes. Grind in processor or blender to coarse powder.

Grease baking sheet. Place sugar in heavy small saucepan. Pour in water to cover. Cook over low heat until sugar melts, shaking pan occasionally. Increase heat and cook without stirring until sugar caramelizes and turns rich mahogany brown, washing down any crystals on sides of pan with brush dipped in cold water. Stir in ground almonds and quickly pour onto baking sheet, smoothing with metal spatula.

Before praline sets, press small fluted cutter in to make 4 flowers (cut several extra in case of breakage), making sure each flower outline is well etched. When praline is completely hard, cut out flowers using sharp knife. Grind remaining praline into fine powder in processor or blender; set aside.

For mousse: Beat egg yolks and powdered sugar until thick and pale yellow and mixture forms a ribbon when beaters are lifted. Beat in amaretto and orange juice. Transfer to heavy saucepan or double boiler and whisk over low heat several minutes until mixture is very thick and you can see bottom of pan between strokes. Remove from heat and beat until cool.

Beat cream in chilled bowl until stiff. Stir ¼ of cream into yolk mixture to loosen. Gently fold in remainder. Cover and refrigerate several hours or overnight.

Spoon mousse into 4 goblets, dividing with several thin layers reserved ground praline and toasted almonds. Leave at least an inch of clearance at top of glass.

For caramel: Combine sugar and corn syrup in small saucepan and cook over medium heat until caramel colored; do not stir, but gently swirl ingredients in pan to mix. *(If sugar crystals form on side of pan, cover and boil rapidly for 2 minutes; steam will wash crystals down sides of pan.)* Syrup should be a rich caramel color. Remove from heat just before desired color is reached as syrup will continue to darken and thicken as it cools. Let cool several minutes.

Dip fork into mixture and slowly drizzle thin threads over mousse. Top each with reserved praline flower. Before serving, let stand in cool place (do not refrigerate) for at least 15 minutes.

Biscuit Tortoni

Can be made up to 3 weeks ahead, wrapped tightly in aluminum foil and frozen.

12 servings

¼ cup amaretto
1 teaspoon unflavored gelatin

4 egg yolks

¼ cup water
½ cup sugar

1 cup whipping cream, whipped
½ cup chopped toasted almonds
¼ cup crushed almond macaroons
Candied fruit *or* sliced almonds, toasted (garnish)

Combine amaretto and gelatin in heat-resistant cup and mix until gelatin is softened. Place cup in simmering water and heat until gelatin is completely liquefied, about 2 to 3 minutes.

Beat egg yolks in large bowl of electric mixer until light and lemon colored.

Combine water and sugar in medium saucepan and bring to boil over medium-high heat, stirring until sugar is completely dissolved. Reduce heat and cook until syrup registers 230°F on candy thermometer, about 5 minutes.

With mixer at low speed, slowly add hot syrup to egg yolks in steady stream, beating until well blended. Add gelatin mixture and continue beating until thick, about 6 minutes. Let cool.

Gently fold whipped cream, almonds and macaroons into mixture. Spoon into 12 foil-lined paper cups. Chill. Before serving, decorate with candied fruit or sliced toasted almonds.

Spumante Cream (Crema alla Spumante)

This is a variation of one of Italy's most delectable contributions to dessert—the zabaglione. Spumante Cream is just as smooth and delicate and can be made ahead. Serve with crisp pinocchiate or amaretti cookies.

8 servings

1 tablespoon unflavored gelatin
¼ cup cold water
1 cup Asti Spumante, room temperature
6 egg yolks, room temperature

½ cup sugar

1 cup whipping cream
16 fresh strawberries *or* fresh raspberries

Sprinkle gelatin over cold water in small bowl and set aside until softened, about 5 minutes. Meanwhile, bring water in bottom of double boiler to simmer over medium heat. Combine wine, yolks and sugar in top of large double boiler. Place over water and whisk until mixture doubles in volume, is pale yellow and forms a thick, heavy ribbon when whisk is lifted, about 20 minutes. Add gelatin and whisk until completely dissolved, about 2 minutes. Remove pan from heat and set on rack to cool, whisking occasionally.

Beat cream to soft peaks in large bowl. Gently but thoroughly fold cream into wine mixture. Drop 1 berry into each of 8 sherbet or wine glasses. Divide Spumante Cream evenly among glasses. Refrigerate at least 2½ hours or overnight. Top each with 1 berry. Serve chilled.

3 ❦ Soufflés

There is nothing quite so light and fluffy as a cloud. Bright and billowy, clouds drift insouciantly through the skies above and through the less limited skies of poets' imaginations. Clouds are wonderful, certainly, except for one small problem: You can't eat them.

But you can eat soufflés.

These airy classics are very nearly as light as clouds, and considerably easier to reach. They are remarkably simple to create; all you need is eggs, cream, or fruit puree, a little sugar and a good oven. And one of the most appealing things about soufflés is their myriad flavoring possibilities: A variety of fruits, liqueurs, and nuts, as well as coffee and chocolate, can turn one basic recipe into a veritable encyclopedia of desserts.

The recipes in this chapter are divided into two categories: cold and hot. Cold soufflés offer the advantage of do-ahead preparation; hot ones naturally require a little last-minute attention, but the results are more than worth it. The ingredients of each type are equally tempting. Here, for example, there are hot and cold versions of pumpkin soufflé, too good to be restricted to the fall holidays. There are combinations of fruit—apple and apricot, orange and lemon juice, apricot and pear, strawberry and raspberry—as well as a number of concoctions in which a single fruit is the star. And for the perfect ending to a sophisticated dinner, there are soufflés based on chocolate, mocha, cappuccino and several popular liqueurs such as amaretto and Irish Mist.

Like Niagara, soufflés are famous for their falls. Do not trust a cook who claims never to have had a soufflé that failed: That person either leads a rich fantasy life or has made a deal with the devil. But there is really no trick to soufflés. As with many other simple dishes, such as omelets, they just require a little practice and patience. Follow the tips and hints in this chapter, try a few of the recipes and soon your appreciative guests will—like clouds—be floating on air.

 Cold Soufflés

Frozen Lemon Frost Soufflé

The meltingly smooth and creamy "crust" contains an airy soufflé-like filling. This cooling dessert is perfect after a substantial meal. Nice with crisp ginger or butter cookies.

8 to 10 servings

Butter and sugar

2 cups whipping cream
Crème Pâtissière (see following recipe)
1 cup strained fresh lemon juice

7 egg whites, room temperature

¼ teaspoon cream of tartar
¼ teaspoon salt
1 cup plus 1 tablespoon sugar

Lemon leaves (garnish)
Candied orange and lemon, slivered (garnish)

Cut strip of foil long enough to wrap around 1½-quart soufflé dish. Fold in half lengthwise. Generously butter 1 side and sprinkle with sugar. Wrap around dish, letting foil extend about 4 inches above rim. Secure with string.

Whip cream in large bowl until soft peaks form. Fold in Crème Pâtissière and lemon juice and set aside.

Whip egg whites in separate bowl until foamy. Add cream of tartar and salt and continue beating until soft peaks form. Gradually add sugar, beating constantly until mixture is stiff and shiny.

Carefully fold whites into lemon-crème mixture until completely incorporated. Spoon into prepared dish. Swirl top using back of spoon or spatula. Carefully cover top with foil. Freeze until quite firm but not solid, about 6 hours. Remove collar and set dish on platter lined with lemon leaves. Garnish with candied orange and lemon slivers.

Crème Pâtissière

Crème can be covered and stored in refrigerator several days before using, if desired. Bring to room temperature and whisk until loosened before using in soufflé.

Makes about 1 cup

2 egg yolks
½ cup sugar
1 tablespoon plus 1 teaspoon all purpose flour

1 cup milk, heated to just below boiling point

¼ teaspoon vanilla

Place yolks in deep small saucepan and beat with whisk until light and frothy. Gradually add sugar, beating constantly until mixture is thick and lemon colored and forms a ribbon when whisk is lifted. Add flour and beat until smooth. Add hot milk a little at a time, beating constantly until well blended.

Place saucepan over medium heat and cook, stirring constantly with whisk, until mixture is thick and coats spoon, about 5 to 6 minutes. (Be sure whisk reaches bottom and sides of pan to prevent lumping or scorching.) Pour into bowl and stir in vanilla. Cool slightly, then cover and chill.

Cold Lime Soufflé

8 to 10 servings

1 cup sugar
¼ cup water
7 egg yolks

½ cup fresh lime juice, or to taste

2 cups (1 pint) whipping cream, whipped
Green food coloring (optional)

Combine sugar and water in medium saucepan and cook over medium-high heat until syrup reaches soft ball stage (235°F on candy thermometer). Mix egg yolks in blender. With machine running at highest speed, add sugar mixture in slow steady stream and mix well. Transfer to large bowl of electric mixer and beat at medium speed until cool.

Add lime juice to egg mixture and blend well. Gently fold in whipped cream. (Add green food coloring if more intense color is desired.) Pour mixture into small soufflé dishes and freeze until serving time.

Orange Marmalade Soufflé

6 to 8 servings

¼ cup Grand Marnier
1 tablespoon fresh lemon juice
3 teaspoons unflavored gelatin

5 eggs, separated
1 cup sugar
¾ cup fresh orange juice
⅓ cup orange marmalade
¼ teaspoon salt
½ teaspoon finely grated lemon peel
1 cup whipping cream

Garnish
½ cup whipping cream
2 teaspoons powdered sugar
½ cup mandarin orange segments, drained
Grand Marnier Sauce (see following recipe)

Prepare 1-quart soufflé dish with lightly oiled 1-inch waxed paper collar. Set aside.

Combine Grand Marnier and lemon juice in small bowl. Sprinkle gelatin over top and let stand until softened.

Combine egg yolks, ¾ cup sugar, orange juice, marmalade and salt in top of double boiler. Set over simmering water and cook, whisking constantly until mixture thickens and coats spoon, about 5 minutes. Remove from heat. Stir in softened gelatin and lemon peel. Turn into large bowl. Let custard cool to room temperature.

Beat egg whites until foamy. Gradually add remaining ¼ cup sugar and continue beating until stiff peaks form. In another bowl, whip 1 cup cream until soft peaks form. Stir some of whites into cooled custard to lighten, then fold in remaining whites, blending well. Fold in whipped cream. Turn into prepared dish. Refrigerate until soufflé is firm and spongy.

For garnish: Whip remaining cream with powdered sugar until stiff. Spoon into pastry bag fitted with star tip. Pipe rosettes over top of soufflé. Decorate with orange segments. Serve with Grand Marnier Sauce.

Grand Marnier Sauce

2 cups milk
¼ cup (½ stick) butter
⅓ cup sugar

3 egg yolks, room temperature
⅓ cup sugar
2 tablespoons cornstarch

1 teaspoon vanilla
⅓ cup Grand Marnier
⅓ cup whipping cream

Combine milk, butter and ⅓ cup sugar in medium saucepan over medium heat and bring to boil, stirring occasionally.

Using electric mixer, beat yolks and remaining sugar in small bowl until thickened. Add cornstarch and continue beating until mixture is light and lemon colored. Gradually beat in enough hot milk to warm mixture slightly. Strain into remaining milk, whisking until blended. Place over medium heat and bring to boil. Remove from heat and stir in vanilla. Let stand until cool. Refrigerate until ready to serve. Just before serving, cook over low heat, stirring in Grand Marnier and whipping cream.

Iced Pear and Apricot Soufflé with Raspberry Sauce

12 servings

2 29-ounce cans pear halves, well drained
2 envelopes unflavored gelatin

½ cup sugar
4 egg yolks
10 dried small apricots (1 ounce total), finely minced
Peel of 2 lemons

3 tablespoons pear brandy
2 tablespoons fresh lemon juice

6 egg whites
⅛ teaspoon salt
¼ cup sugar
Raspberry Sauce (see following recipe)

Cut piece of foil long enough to encircle 5- to 6-cup soufflé dish with 1-inch overlap. Fold in half lengthwise. Oil one side. Wrap around dish oiled side in with collar extending at least 4 inches above rim. Tie or tape firmly.

Cut 2 pear halves into ¼-inch dice; set aside. Puree remaining pears with gelatin in processor or blender in batches. Transfer to large saucepan and cook over medium heat until reduced to about 1 cup, about 45 minutes.

Combine ½ cup sugar with egg yolks, apricots and lemon peel in processor or large bowl of electric mixer and blend until mixture is thick and pale yellow. Add 2 tablespoons hot pear puree and blend well. Add remaining puree with brandy and lemon juice and mix thoroughly. Transfer to large bowl and fold in diced pears. Refrigerate until mixture begins to thicken.

Beat egg whites with electric mixer until foamy. Add salt and continue beating until whites are stiff and glossy. Add remaining ¼ cup sugar and beat 5 seconds. Stir ¼ of whites into pear mixture and mix well. Fold in remaining whites, blending gently but thoroughly. Spoon into prepared dish. Refrigerate until completely set, several hours or overnight. Serve with Raspberry Sauce.

Raspberry Sauce

Makes about 1 cup

1 10-ounce package frozen raspberries, thawed (undrained)

1 tablespoon kirsch (optional)

Pulverize raspberries in processor or blender for at least 1 minute. Strain if desired. Stir in kirsch. Cover and chill until ready to serve.

Amaretto Peaches
Filled with Amaretto Zabaglione

Brian Leatart

*From left: Red and Purple Plums in Spiced Wine,
Poppy Seed Cookies, Raspberry Poached Pears,
Marsala Baked Apples*

Clockwise from left: Langues des Chats,
Vanilla Almond Crescents, Cinnamon Stars,
Dentelles, Fondant-dipped Strawberries

*From left: Cold Pumpkin Soufflé,
Moustache Cafe Chocolate Soufflé*

Brian Leatart

Lemon Soufflé in Lemon Shells

Cold Pumpkin Soufflé

6 servings

¼ cup ginger-flavored brandy
1 envelope unflavored gelatin

4 egg yolks
⅔ cup sugar
1 16-ounce can pumpkin
1 teaspoon freshly grated orange peel
1 teaspoon cinnamon
½ teaspoon ground ginger
¼ teaspoon mace

¼ teaspoon ground cloves

4 egg whites
1 cup whipping cream, whipped

½ cup chopped toasted walnuts, pecans *or* almonds, *or* crumbled English toffee
1 pint vanilla ice cream
2 tablespoons frozen orange juice concentrate, thawed

Oil 6-inch-wide band of waxed paper and tie around 1-quart soufflé dish to form collar extending about 2 inches above rim.

Pour brandy in top of double boiler. Sprinkle with gelatin and set over simmering water. Stir constantly until gelatin is completely dissolved.

Combine yolks and ½ cup sugar in medium bowl and beat until thick and pale yellow. Blend in pumpkin, orange peel, cinnamon, ginger, mace and cloves. Mix in dissolved gelatin.

Beat egg whites in medium bowl until soft peaks form. Gradually add remaining sugar and beat until stiff and glossy. Fold into pumpkin mixture, then fold in whipped cream. Spoon into soufflé dish and chill until set, at least 8 hours.

Carefully remove collar. Decorate soufflé with border of nuts or toffee. Let ice cream soften slightly and blend with orange juice concentrate. Serve separately as sauce for soufflé.

Tangerine Soufflé with Mandarin Sauce

8 to 10 servings

Tangerine Soufflé
4 extra-large egg yolks
1½ cups milk, scalded
3 ounces cream cheese, room temperature, cut into ½-inch cubes
1 tablespoon grated tangerine peel
½ cup sugar
Pinch of salt
1½ envelopes unflavored gelatin softened in ½ cup Mandarine Napoléon (tangerine liqueur)
8 ounces frozen tangerine concentrate, thawed
1 tablespoon fresh lemon juice

1 cup whipping cream, well chilled

4 extra-large egg whites
¼ cup sugar
Pinch of salt
Pinch of cream of tartar

Mandarin Sauce
3 extra-large or 2 jumbo egg yolks
2 tablespoons sugar
4 tablespoons (¼ cup) Mandarine Napoléon (tangerine liqueur)
½ cup whipping cream

For soufflé: Prepare eight to ten 2½ × 1½-inch soufflé dishes by cutting strip of foil long enough to wrap around each dish with some overlap. Fold in half lengthwise. Generously butter 1 side and sprinkle with sugar. Wrap around dishes, buttered side in, letting foil extend 2 inches above rims. Secure with string. Refrigerate dishes.

Beat egg yolks in large bowl of electric mixer at medium speed. With mixer running, gradually add milk in slow steady stream, beating constantly until well blended. Add cream cheese and grated tangerine peel and beat until smooth. Transfer mixture to double boiler set over simmering water. Add sugar and salt and whisk until mixture thickens and coats spoon. Remove from heat. Add gelatin mixture and stir until dissolved. Mix in tangerine concentrate and lemon juice. Chill until mixture begins to set.

Meanwhile, whip 1 cup cream in small bowl of electric mixer until soft peaks hold their shape. Refrigerate.

Beat egg whites in large bowl of electric mixer at low speed just until foam appears around edge of bowl. Gradually increase speed of mixer and slowly add sugar, beating until whites are nearly stiff. Add salt and cream of tartar and beat until whites are stiff but not dry.

Whisk chilled tangerine mixture until smooth, then gently fold in whipped cream. Fold in ¼ of egg whites, blending well. Add remaining whites, folding until completely incorporated. Spoon evenly into prepared soufflé dishes. Chill until set, 4 to 6 hours.

For sauce: Combine egg yolks and sugar in top of double boiler set over boiling water and whisk until thick and lemon colored. Remove from heat. Stir in 2 tablespoons tangerine liqueur. Immediately set saucepan in bowl of ice water to cool, then refrigerate until well chilled. Beat whipping cream in chilled bowl just until thickened. Gently fold whipped cream into egg mixture. Stir in remaining 2 tablespoons liqueur.

To serve, remove collars from soufflé dishes. Tie narrow, decorative ribbon around each dish and arrange on large platter. Serve sauce separately.

Persimmon Soufflé Roll

8 servings

Persimmon Soufflé
    Butter and powdered sugar

½ **cup (2 ounces) blanched almonds**

3 **medium persimmons (14 ounces total)**
2 **tablespoons fresh lemon juice**
1 **tablespoon Grand Marnier**
1 **tablespoon finely grated orange peel**

6 **egg yolks, room temperature**
½ **cup (8 tablespoons) sugar**

6 **egg whites, room temperature**
    Pinch of salt
    Pinch of cream of tartar

Persimmon Filling
3 **small persimmons (10½ ounces total)**
1 **tablespoon fresh lemon juice**
½ **cup sugar**

1 **cup whipping cream**
2 **tablespoons Grand Marnier**

½ **cup (2 ounces) sliced almonds, toasted (garnish)**
8 **glacéed apricots (garnish)**
    Autumn leaves (optional garnish)

For soufflé: Preheat oven to 375°F. Line 12 × 18-inch jelly roll pan with sheet of buttered parchment or waxed paper, extending paper several inches beyond edges of pan. Dust lightly with powdered sugar, shaking off excess.

Toast blanched almonds and grind finely in processor or blender; remove and set aside.

Halve persimmons; discard seeds. Scoop 1 cup pulp into processor or blender. Add lemon juice and Grand Marnier and puree, stopping to scrape sides of container. Mix in orange peel.

Place egg yolks in medium mixing bowl. Gradually beat in 6 tablespoons sugar and beat until yolks are thick, lemon colored and form a ribbon when beaters are lifted, about 3 to 5 minutes. Gently fold in ground almonds and persimmon puree.

Beat egg whites in large bowl until foamy. Add salt and cream of tartar and continue beating until soft peaks form. Sprinkle with remaining 2 tablespoons sugar 1 tablespoon at a time and continue beating until stiff but not dry. Stir ¼ of whites into yolk mixture, then fold back into remaining whites.

Turn into prepared pan, spreading evenly with spatula. Bake until puffed and brown, about 15 minutes. Let cool 10 minutes, then cover with plastic wrap. Let stand at room temperature until completely cool, 2 to 3 hours.

For filling: Halve persimmons; discard seeds. Scoop ¾ cup pulp into processor or blender. Add lemon juice and puree, stopping to scrape down sides of container. Transfer to heavy small saucepan and blend in sugar. Cook over low heat, stirring occasionally until sugar is dissolved, then increase heat to medium high and continue cooking, stirring frequently, until mixture thickens and jells enough to fall slowly from spoon in droplets, about 10 to 15 minutes. Let cool to room temperature.

Discard plastic wrap from soufflé. Carefully remove soufflé and parchment paper from pan. Run spatula under soufflé to be sure it doesn't stick to paper; trim any hard edges.

Beat cream with remaining 2 tablespoons Grand Marnier until thick. Fold in ¾ of persimmon filling. Spread over soufflé, leaving 1-inch border on all sides. Using paper as guide, very carefully roll up soufflé and transfer seam side down to long serving platter. Spread remaining ¼ of persimmon filling over outside of roll. Refrigerate for several hours.

Let stand at room temperature 30 minutes before serving. Garnish with almonds and apricots and with autumn leaves if desired.

Chilled Fresh Peach Yogurt Soufflé

The texture of this soufflé is best when served the same day it is prepared. Use the dried apricots if peaches are out of season. You may also substitute 2 cups pureed nectarines, strawberries or raspberries for the pureed peaches.

6 to 8 servings

Soufflé
- ½ cup fresh orange juice
- 2 envelopes unflavored gelatin
- 8 dried apricots (optional)
- 1½ pounds ripe peaches, peeled and pitted (2 cups pureed)
- ½ cup sugar, or less if fruit is very sweet
- 1 tablespoon kirsch
- 1½ cups plain yogurt
- 4 large egg whites

- ¼ cup sugar

Garnishes
- 1 small peach, unpeeled and thinly sliced
- ½ teaspoon fresh lemon juice
- 1 teaspoon sugar
- 1 teaspoon kirsch
- ½ cup whipping cream
- 1 teaspoon sugar

For soufflé: Prepare 1-quart soufflé dish. Make collar by cutting piece of foil long enough to encircle dish with 2-inch overlap. Fold foil in half lengthwise, oil one side and place around dish, extending 2 inches above edge. Tie or tape firmly around edge of dish.

Mix orange juice and gelatin in glass measuring cup; let stand until gelatin has absorbed all liquid. Melt gelatin by setting cup in boiling water, or microwave 2 minutes on Defrost or Medium setting. If using apricots, either simmer covered in ¼ cup water about 10 minutes, or microwave, covered, on High, in ¼ cup water 3 minutes.

Chop apricots and peaches, then puree in processor or blender in batches, stopping once to scrape down sides of container with spatula. Add ½ cup sugar, melted gelatin and kirsch and mix until completely blended. Fold yogurt into mixture and blend thoroughly. (*Overbeating will cause yogurt to liquefy.*)

With electric mixer, beat egg whites until foamy. Gradually add remaining ¼ cup sugar and beat until stiff, but not dry. Carefully fold in ¼ of peach mixture, then fold in remaining mixture. Spoon mixture into prepared dish and refrigerate at least 4 hours.

For garnishes: Mix peach slices with lemon juice, sugar and kirsch and set aside. Lightly whip cream, adding sugar just before cream is completely thickened. Place cream in pastry bag fitted with medium star tip and decorate soufflé. Carefully drain peach slices and arrange on soufflé. Serve immediately.

Frozen Raspberry Soufflé

If fresh raspberries are unavailable, use slightly thawed frozen berries and chop coarsely in processor or blender.

8 servings

1 pint lightly sweetened fresh raspberries *or* 1 10-ounce package frozen raspberries, thawed and undrained Framboise *or* kirsch

1 cup sugar
1 cup water
1 tablespoon corn syrup

3 egg whites
1 8-inch génoise *or* sponge cake, split into 3 layers horizontally and cut into 1- to 1½-inch pieces

½ cup whipping cream, whipped

1 cup raspberry syrup
1 cup fresh raspberries

Prepare 1-quart soufflé dish with lightly oiled 3-inch waxed paper collar, securing with string. Set aside. Sprinkle berries lightly with framboise or kirsch.

Combine sugar, water and corn syrup in small saucepan. Bring to boil over medium heat, stirring frequently just until sugar dissolves. Continue boiling, without stirring, to soft ball stage (235°F on candy thermometer). Remove from heat.

Using electric mixer, beat egg whites until soft peaks form. Gradually add ¾ cup syrup, beating constantly until whites are stiff and shiny. Flavor remaining syrup with framboise and drizzle evenly over cake.

Gently fold berries into meringue, then fold in whipped cream. Spoon generous layer of raspberry mixture into prepared soufflé dish and top with about half of cake. Repeat, ending with raspberry mixture (soufflé should almost reach top of collar). Freeze several hours.

Meanwhile, combine raspberry syrup with framboise to taste. Add about 1 cup raspberries and blend well.

Transfer soufflé to refrigerator 1 to 1½ hours before serving. Carefully remove collar just before bringing soufflé to table. Serve sauce separately.

Frozen Strawberry Soufflé

12 to 16 servings

6 large eggs, separated
1 cup sugar
2 cups strawberry puree
½ cup Grand Marnier

1 cup sugar
⅓ cup fresh orange juice

3 cups whipping cream

Walnut halves *or* pistachios
½ cup whipping cream
Whole strawberries
Raspberry Sauce (see following recipe)

In large bowl beat egg yolks until thick and lemon colored. Add 1 cup sugar and beat until dissolved. Stir in ½ cup strawberry puree. Place in top of double boiler and cook over hot water until thickened, about 15 to 20 minutes, stirring frequently. Allow to cool. Add Grand Marnier a little at a time until thoroughly blended. Set aside.

Combine 1 cup sugar and orange juice in 1-quart saucepan. Cook, uncovered, over medium-low heat, stirring until dissolved. Continue cooking without stirring until mixture reaches soft ball stage (235°F on candy thermometer).

While orange juice and sugar are cooking, beat egg whites until soft peaks form. Very slowly pour in hot orange syrup, beating until stiff peaks form.

Whip cream and fold into yolk mixture. Fold in remaining strawberry puree. Gently but thoroughly fold in meringue. Spoon into oiled and collared 1½-quart soufflé dish. Freeze about 1½ to 2 hours. When firm, carefully wrap in freezer paper, securing edges with masking tape.

To serve, remove collar and press walnuts or pistachios around sides or top of soufflé. Whip cream and use to garnish top. Decorate with strawberries and serve with Raspberry Sauce.

Raspberry Sauce

Makes about 3 cups

3 10-ounce packages frozen raspberries, thawed and undrained

¼ cup Grand Marnier

Combine ingredients in blender and puree. Strain if desired.

Irish Mist Soufflé

2 servings

1 egg, separated
2 tablespoons superfine sugar
1 teaspoon unflavored gelatin
1 tablespoon Irish Mist liqueur

¼ cup whipping cream, whipped
1 tablespoon sliced almonds, toasted

Beat yolk with sugar until light and fluffy. Melt gelatin with liqueur in small bowl over simmering water. Beat yolk mixture into gelatin until thoroughly combined. Remove from heat.

In another bowl, beat egg white until stiff. Fold into gelatin mixture and allow to stand until slightly thickened. Fold in whipped cream, then nuts. Spoon into individual dessert dishes or wine glasses and chill several hours.

Frozen Amaretto Soufflé

8 servings

Butter and sugar

1½ cups sugar
6 eggs, room temperature
6 egg yolks, room temperature

3 tablespoons amaretto
3 cups whipping cream

Fresh fruit (garnish)
Mint sprigs (garnish)

Prepare collar for 2-quart soufflé dish by cutting strip of foil long enough to wrap around dish with some overlap. Fold in half lengthwise. Generously butter 1 side and sprinkle with sugar. Wrap around dish, buttered side in, letting foil extend 3½ inches above rim. Secure tightly with string.

Add 1½ cups sugar, eggs and yolks to top of double boiler set over warm (*not hot*) water over low heat and stir constantly with whisk or rubber spatula until just warm, about 12 minutes. Transfer egg mixture to large bowl of electric mixer and beat until stiff, about 10 minutes. Blend in amaretto. Whip cream in another large bowl until soft peaks form. Gently fold cream into egg mixture, blending well. Pour soufflé into prepared dish. Freeze until firm, at least 5 hours.

Before serving, let soufflé soften in refrigerator 15 minutes. Spoon soufflé onto individual plates. Garnish with fresh fruit and mint sprigs.

 Hot Soufflés

Apple-Apricot Soufflé

2 servings

Butter and sugar

1 large tart apple (8 ounces), peeled, cored and thinly sliced
1 tablespoon apricot preserves
1 teaspoon water
Pinch of cinnamon

2 tablespoons sugar, or more
1 egg yolk

1 tablespoon all purpose flour
¼ cup milk, scalded
1 tablespoon dark rum
2 teaspoons butter
1 teaspoon vanilla

2 egg whites, room temperature
Pinch of salt
Powdered sugar (garnish)

Generously butter two 1-cup soufflé dishes and sprinkle with sugar.

Combine apple, apricot preserves, water and cinnamon in heavy small saucepan. Cover and cook over medium-low heat until mixture forms thick puree, 20 to 25 minutes. Cool.

Preheat oven to 425°F. Combine 2 tablespoons sugar, yolk and flour in medium saucepan and whisk to blend. Stir in hot milk. Bring to boil over medium heat, stirring constantly. Reduce heat and simmer gently 2 minutes, stirring constantly. Remove from heat and blend in rum, butter and vanilla. Fold in apple. Add sugar if necessary.

Beat whites with salt in medium bowl until stiff. Fold ¼ of whites into apple mixture, then gently fold in remaining whites. Divide soufflé mixture between prepared dishes. Bake until puffed and browned, about 10 to 15 minutes. Immediately sift powdered sugar lightly over top and serve.

Lemon Soufflé in Lemon Shells

Each serving consists of 2 soufflé-filled lemon cups.

6 servings

6 large lemons

3 egg yolks
4 tablespoons sugar
3 tablespoons fresh lemon juice
Grated peel of 1 lemon

4 egg whites
¼ teaspoon salt
1 tablespoon sugar

Preheat oven to 375°F. Slice ends from lemons so they will set level. Halve horizontally either straight across or in a zigzag design, making 12 small lemon cups. Remove pulp, being careful not to pierce the shell. Drain shells upside down on paper towels.

Beat egg yolks with 4 tablespoons sugar until thick and light yellow. Add lemon juice and peel.

Beat whites with salt until they form soft peaks. Add remaining 1 tablespoon sugar and continue beating until stiff. Fold whites into yolk mixture.

Fill 12 lemon cups with soufflé mixture. Place in 9 × 13-inch dish and bake until lightly browned, about 15 minutes.

Mandarin Soufflé

These little soufflés will not collapse. If tangerines are not in season, use Valencia oranges.

6 servings

8 medium tangerines
2 tablespoons Grand Marnier

2 egg yolks
3 tablespoons sugar
2 tablespoons all purpose flour
½ cup nonfat milk, warmed
½ teaspoon fresh lemon juice

1 12-ounce can mandarin orange sections

3 egg whites
½ cup water

Grate zest (colored portion of citrus peel with no membrane—use light touch when grating) of 1 tangerine and chop very fine. Place in small saucepan over low heat with 1 tablespoon Grand Marnier; heat until liqueur has evaporated.

Cut off top third of 7 remaining tangerines (halve if using oranges). Remove flesh carefully, leaving shells intact for filling. Push pulp through fine strainer, reserving juice. Set aside 6 shells.

Beat egg yolks with 2½ tablespoons sugar in medium bowl until mixture thickens and is very pale in color. Stir in flour. Gradually add warm milk. Transfer mixture to a heavy-bottomed small pan; place over low heat and whisk until custard thickens, approximately 10 minutes. Gradually add ½ cup tangerine juice and continue to whisk until custard thickens again. Remove from heat and force through fine strainer. Cool before adding remaining 1 tablespoon Grand Marnier and lemon juice.

Drain mandarin sections; cut into small pieces. Combine with ⅔ of the strained custard. Add tangerine zest. Spoon into reserved tangerine shells, dividing equally.

Preheat oven to 325°F. Beat egg whites until soft peaks form. Add remaining ½ tablespoon sugar and continue beating until quite stiff. Fold in reserved custard. Place in pastry bag fitted with ⅓-inch star tube. Pipe meringue into tangerine shells, mounding it in circular fashion. Arrange tangerines in shallow baking dish with ½ cup water. Bake until lightly browned, about 20 minutes.

🍮 Simple Steps to Spectacular Soufflés

Don't believe all of those stories you've heard about how difficult it is to make a dessert soufflé. Actually, there are only a few basic points to keep in mind for a picture-perfect, high-rising soufflé. And they're easy to master.

The utensils. All you need is a whisk or mixer, a mixing bowl and a soufflé dish. But your choice of utensil will contribute to your soufflé's success.

- **The whisk.** Whisking the egg whites by hand incorporates more air bubbles into them and yields a loftier soufflé. If you must use an electric mixer for beating the egg whites, it is a good idea to add a pinch of sugar or cream of tartar or a drop of lemon juice to the mixture. This will help increase the volume and stabilize the whites.

- **The mixing bowl.** As with the whisk, history, tradition and testing dictate what is best: In this case it's a copper-lined bowl. A harmless chemical reaction with the copper strengthens the bubbles in the beaten egg whites. Stainless steel bowls will also work well, but avoid using aluminum, which can cause discoloration, or plastic or glass, which, because of their slippery sides, can allow unbeaten whites to slip to the bottom.

- **The soufflé dish.** The traditional round, high-sided containers can be found in a variety of sizes. But any ovenproof, straight-sided dish will do the job. Take note, though, that cooking times may vary according to the size you choose, so keep a close eye on the soufflé.

Egg whites—the most important element. It is the supposed delicacy of beaten egg whites that gives soufflés the reputation for being difficult. With some simple precautions, however, you'll prepare them with ease.

- Beat the egg whites *just before* mixing and baking the soufflé, so they won't have time to fall.

- Bring the whites to room temperature before beating.

- Separate the eggs one at a time over a small bowl, to ensure that not a speck of yolk mixes with the whites.

- Make sure the mixing bowl is completely clean and dry before adding the egg whites.

Brandied Pumpkin Soufflé

This delicious dessert can also be served as a side dish with holiday menus.

6 servings

2 cups pumpkin puree
½ cup hot milk
¼ cup brandy
¼ cup (½ stick) butter, room temperature
4½ tablespoons sugar
½ teaspoon freshly grated nutmeg
Pinch of cinnamon

Pinch of salt
4 eggs, separated, room temperature
1 teaspoon finely grated lemon peel

Pinch of cream of tartar
1½ tablespoons sugar

- Beat the whites as gently as possible until stiff but not dry. They should form soft peaks and cling to the sides of the mixing bowl.

The soufflé base. This thick, creamy mixture gives the soufflé its flavor and richness. It usually includes egg yolks, milk or other liquids, flavorings such as liqueurs, extracts, fruit or fruit juices and sometimes flour.

- The base can be made well ahead of time, covered and refrigerated, or left at room temperature until it's needed. If you do refrigerate the base, remember to bring it to room temperature before incorporating the whites.
- If the base sauce seems heavy or thick, blend in ¼ to ½ cup of the beaten egg whites to lighten it before you add the rest.
- Fold (*never* stir or beat) the egg whites into the sauce. This is often easier if you do it in two stages: Fold in the first half gently to thoroughly incorporate the two mixtures. Then fold in the second half: Don't worry if some "unflavored" patches of white remain.

Preparing the soufflé dish and baking. Since dessert soufflés are generally higher and lighter than other soufflés, it is often necessary to attach a waxed paper extension to the soufflé dish to keep the mixture from overflowing. Check your recipe to see what type of collar is needed. Collars are usually buttered so they can easily be removed the moment the soufflé comes out of the oven. Which brings us to the final controversy: Should the soufflé dish be buttered, buttered and sugared or left untreated? Contrary to popular culinary opinion, a buttered dish will not help a soufflé "slide" up the sides of the dish. Sugar will not provide something for a soufflé to "cling" to as it rises. A buttered and sugared dish will, however, give a soufflé a chewy, sweetened crust. And finally, your oven should be carefully preheated and your guests should be waiting at the table when the soufflé comes out. A perfect soufflé waits for no one.

Preheat oven to 400°F. Butter 1-quart soufflé dish. Cut parchment collar with 2-inch overlap for soufflé dish. Butter parchment; wrap around dish buttered side in. Staple or tape ends and tie with string.

Whisk pumpkin puree, hot milk, brandy, butter, 4½ tablespoons sugar, nutmeg, cinnamon and salt in large bowl. Blend in egg yolks and lemon peel.

Beat egg whites with cream of tartar until soft peaks form. Gradually beat in 1½ tablespoons sugar until whites are stiff but not dry. Fold into pumpkin mixture. Pour into prepared dish. Bake until soufflé is well puffed and lightly browned on top, 25 to 30 minutes. Serve immediately.

🍎 *Omelets for Dessert*

The sweet omelet is a delicious answer to the panicky questions that arise when you have 5 minutes to plan and cook dessert. Plain, with just a little sugar and perhaps some grated lemon peel or vanilla to distinguish it from its savory counterpart, it is a wholesome dessert. A luscious filling raises it to a much grander level.

Here are 3 versions of this quick, creamy wonder: the Classic Sweet Omelet, a lightly beaten egg mixture that is cooked over direct heat and folded to enclose a filling; the Puffy Sweet Omelet, for which the yolks and whites are beaten separately, combined and baked, then folded in the same shape as the classic omelet; and the Omelet Soufflé, which is baked in a different shape and is not filled.

If making several omelets, beat the necessary number of eggs and other ingredients together in a bowl and use a measuring cup to pour out the right amount. Two large eggs measure about ⅓ cup; three eggs, ½ cup.

Before serving an omelet, shine its surface with pat of cold butter, sprinkle with powdered sugar or decorate with whipped or sour cream.

Filling Suggestions for Classic and Puffy Sweet Omelets

Fillings for sweet omelets are rolled up inside or spooned on top after the omelet is folded and turned out onto its heated serving platter. To spoon a filling on top, cut a slit down the center of the top surface, leaving a ¾-inch margin at each end. Separate the edges of the slit slightly and spoon the filling between them. The following fillings are good by themselves or can be mixed and matched for countless intriguing variations. Allow about ⅓ cup filling for each omelet.

- Fresh, dried, candied or poached fruits presented sliced, chopped, pureed or marinated in a liqueur
- Toasted whole, sliced or chopped nuts, glacéed nuts or praline
- Melted jam, jelly or preserves
- Maple or fruit syrup
- Whipped cream, sour cream, crème fraîche or pastry cream
- Crushed macaroons or ladyfingers

Classic Sweet Omelet

Firm on the outside and soft, moist and curdy within, this omelet is traditionally cooked in a heavy 6- or 7-inch skillet that has a long handle, sloping sides and non-stick surface.

3 **eggs, room temperature**	1 **tablespoon unsalted butter**
1 **tablespoon sugar**	**Filling (see list)**
1 **teaspoon water** *or* **liqueur**	
½ **teaspoon vanilla**	

Slowly heat omelet pan over medium heat (pan must be sufficiently hot so that dab of butter dropped into it sizzles but does not brown). Gently mix eggs, sugar, water and vanilla until whites and yolks are just combined.

Increase heat to medium high, add butter and tilt pan so butter covers bottom and sides. When butter stops foaming, add eggs all at once. Imme-

Classic Sweet Omelets are usually eaten as soon as they are cooked, but they can also be served at room temperature or re-heated by flaming with 3 tablespoons liqueur.

diately begin to shake pan with one hand while simultaneously using the other hand to stir eggs in circular motion with the flat of fork. At first, fork should touch the bottom of the pan as you stir, so that eggs are moved all around the pan and away from the sides. As eggs begin to set, stir only the surface, always with a circular motion. When eggs are lightly set (omelet must be very soft because it will continue to cook from its own interior heat after it is removed from the pan), make a shallow cut down center of omelet, fill with ⅓ cup of filling, fold over and slide out onto heated serving platter.

Puffy Sweet Omelet

2 to 4 servings

6 eggs, separated, room temperature	2 tablespoons sugar
⅛ teaspoon salt	2 tablespoons (¼ stick) unsalted butter
⅛ teaspoon cream of tartar	Filling (see list)

Preheat oven to 350°F. Beat egg yolks in medium bowl until they are thick, lemon colored and form a ribbon when beaters are lifted. Set aside. Beat egg whites with salt and cream of tartar in large bowl until soft peaks form. Beat in sugar 1 tablespoon at a time and continue beating until whites are stiff and glossy. Gently stir ¼ of whites into yolks, then fold yolks back into whites.

Melt butter in heavy 12-inch skillet over medium-high heat, tilting pan so butter covers bottom and sides. When butter stops foaming, add egg mixture all at once, smoothing with metal spatula. Immediately transfer to oven and bake until omelet is puffed and browned and top feels firm to touch (inside will still be creamy), about 15 minutes. Make shallow cut down center of omelet. Spread ⅔ cup filling over one half and fold over. Slide omelet out onto heated platter and serve.

Omelet Soufflé

4 servings

4 eggs, separated, room temperature	⅛ teaspoon salt
1 tablespoon Grand Marnier	⅛ teaspoon cream of tartar
Finely grated peel of 1 orange	Powdered sugar
½ cup sugar	¼ cup Grand Marnier, heated

Preheat oven to 400°F. Generously butter shallow round baking dish or gratin pan. Beat egg yolks with 1 tablespoon liqueur and orange peel in medium bowl. Gradually add ¼ cup sugar, beating constantly until yolks are thick and lemon colored and mixture forms a ribbon when beaters are lifted. Beat egg whites with salt and cream of tartar in large bowl until soft peaks form. Add remaining ¼ cup sugar 1 tablespoon at a time and continue beating until whites are stiff and glossy. Gently stir ¼ of whites into yolks, then fold yolk mixture back into whites. Spoon mixture evenly into prepared dish (or pipe from pastry bag). Sprinkle with powdered sugar. Bake until soufflé is puffed and browned, about 12 minutes. Remove from oven, ignite heated liqueur and pour over soufflé. Spoon omelet onto heated serving plates.

Hot Orange-Apricot Soufflé

This dessert is well worth the last-minute whipping and folding of egg whites.

8 servings

Butter
1 tablespoon sugar

6 to 7 navel oranges, peel and white membranes removed
1 lemon, peeled

Minced peel of 2 oranges
7 tablespoons sugar
15 dried apricots, chopped
6 tablespoons (¾ stick) unsalted butter

6 large egg yolks
8 large egg whites
¼ teaspoon cream of tartar
¼ teaspoon salt
¼ cup sugar
1 tablespoon powdered sugar (optional)
Orange slices (optional)

Butter inside and edge of 2-quart soufflé dish. Sprinkle with 1 tablespoon sugar. Place collar of buttered waxed paper around dish and tie with string.

Slice 4 oranges; set slices aside. Juice 2 oranges with lemon and strain to obtain ¾ juice (additional juice may be needed). Set aside.

Combine minced orange peel, 7 tablespoons sugar and apricots in processor or blender in batches. Mix thoroughly. Place mixture in saucepan with juice and butter. Heat until butter is melted.

Blend 6 egg yolks until light in processor or with electric mixer. With machine still running, pour hot juice mixture in very slowly. *Mixture can be prepared ahead to this point. Cover and let stand at room temperature.*

Place rack in middle of oven. Preheat oven to 425°F. Beat egg whites until foamy. Add cream of tartar and salt and beat until stiff but not dry. Gently fold in remaining ¼ cup sugar. Fold ¼ of very warm orange mixture (reheated if prepared in advance) into egg whites.

Carefully fold egg whites into remaining mixture. Place in prepared dish using spatula. Bake until soufflé is puffed and very brown, 16 to 17 minutes. Dust with powdered sugar and serve immediately, spooning soft center, which will be like a sauce, over orange slices and outer portion of soufflé.

Moustache Cafe Chocolate Soufflé

6 servings

6 ounces dark sweet chocolate, cut into pieces
½ cup plus 1 teaspoon sugar
⅓ cup milk
4 egg yolks

6 egg whites
¼ cup sugar

Powdered sugar (garnish)

Preheat oven to 350°F. Butter six ½-cup soufflé dishes and sprinkle with sugar, shaking out excess. Combine chocolate, ½ cup plus 1 teaspoon sugar and milk in medium saucepan. Set over low heat and cook, stirring frequently, until chocolate is melted. Transfer to mixing bowl and let cool slightly. Beat in egg yolks.

Beat egg whites in medium bowl until firm. Add remaining sugar and continue beating until whites are stiff and glossy.

Stir half of whites into chocolate mixture, then carefully fold in remaining whites, blending thoroughly. Gently spoon into prepared dishes. Bake 20 minutes. Sprinkle tops with powdered sugar and serve.

Mocha Soufflé

2 servings

2 tablespoons (¼ stick) butter, room temperature
4 tablespoons sugar

1 ounce unsweetened chocolate
1 tablespoon coffee liqueur
⅓ cup milk, scalded
1 tablespoon all purpose flour
¼ teaspoon vanilla
1 egg yolk

2 egg whites
½ cup whipping cream
1 tablespoon coffee liqueur
Sifted powdered sugar

Preheat oven to 375°F. Using 1 tablespoon butter, butter two 1½-cup soufflé dishes. Sprinkle evenly with 1 tablespoon sugar. Set aside.

Heat chocolate, 1 tablespoon liqueur, remaining 3 tablespoons sugar and milk in top of double boiler set over simmering water. Melt remaining 1 tablespoon butter in small saucepan over medium heat. Stir in flour until smooth. Gradually add chocolate mixture, blending thoroughly. Stir in vanilla. Beat in yolk. Remove from heat.

Beat egg whites in small bowl until stiff. Carefully fold into chocolate mixture. Divide between prepared dishes. Bake until soufflé is puffed and springy, about 15 to 20 minutes.

Meanwhile, whip cream until soft peaks form. Add remaining liqueur and continue beating until stiff. Dust top of soufflé with sifted powdered sugar and serve with whipped cream.

Cappuccino Soufflé

8 to 10 servings

Butter and sugar

2 cups milk
2 tablespoons coffee liqueur
2 tablespoons instant coffee powder
1 tablespoon Cognac
½ ounce unsweetened chocolate
Several drops of vanilla

¼ cup (½ stick) unsalted butter
2 rounded tablespoons all purpose flour
¼ cup sugar
Pinch of salt
6 egg yolks

6 egg whites

Preheat oven to 350°F. Butter 1-quart soufflé dish and dust lightly with sugar, shaking out excess. Set dish aside.

Combine milk, liqueur, coffee powder, Cognac, chocolate and vanilla in medium saucepan over low heat and cook, stirring frequently, until chocolate is melted. Remove from heat and set aside.

Melt ¼ cup butter in 2-quart saucepan over medium heat. Add flour and stir until bubbly. Gradually add chocolate mixture, sugar and salt, whisking constantly until smooth. Bring to boil and cook until thickened, about 2 to 3 minutes. Turn into large bowl. Add egg yolks 1 at a time, whisking until well blended.

Beat egg whites in another bowl until stiff and glossy. Stir large spoonful of whites into chocolate mixture to lighten. Fold in remaining whites until completely incorporated. Gently spoon into prepared dish, mounding slightly in center. Bake until tester inserted near center of soufflé comes out clean, about 25 minutes.

Hazelnut Soufflé with Mixed Fruit Sauce

12 servings

Sauce
1½ cups 1-inch pineapple cubes
    (about ¼ fresh pineapple)
1½ cups muscat dessert wine
 ½ pound (about 2 cups)
    strawberries, hulled
 ½ cup whipping cream
1½ tablespoons hazelnut liqueur

Soufflé
 Butter and sugar

1½ cups milk
 ½ cup sugar
 ¼ cup finely minced husked and
    toasted hazelnuts
 ¼ cup (½ stick) unsalted butter
 ¼ cup all purpose flour
 6 eggs, separated, room
    temperature
 2 tablespoons hazelnut liqueur

For sauce: Combine pineapple and wine in large saucepan over low heat. Cover and cook until very soft but not mushy, 45 to 60 minutes. Add strawberries and simmer 2 to 3 minutes, stirring and mashing fruit as much as possible. Press fruit mixture through sieve set over bowl. Transfer puree to saucepan. Place over high heat and reduce to 1 cup, 2 to 3 minutes. Add cream and liqueur and stir constantly 1 minute. Set sauce aside.

For soufflé: Preheat oven to 400°F. Butter 2-quart soufflé dish. Sprinkle with sugar, shaking out excess. Prepare collar by cutting strip of foil long enough to wrap around dish, allowing 1-inch overlap. Cut foil about 7 inches wide. Fold in half lengthwise. Butter and sugar 1 side of foil, shaking off excess. Wrap around dish. Secure with string.

Scald milk with sugar and hazelnuts in large saucepan over medium-high heat, stirring to dissolve sugar, 4 to 5 minutes. Melt butter in medium saucepan over low heat. Add flour and whisk 2 to 3 minutes; do not let flour brown. Blend in milk mixture, stirring until smooth and thick. Remove from heat. Whisk in yolks 2 at a time, blending after each addition. Stir in liqueur.

Beat egg whites in large bowl until stiff but not dry. Stir about ¼ of whites into yolk mixture to lighten. Gently fold in remaining whites. Pour batter into prepared dish. Bake until puffed and cooked through, 30 to 35 minutes. Serve soufflé immediately. Serve sauce separately.

4 ❧ Iced Desserts

Fashions in desserts, like fashions in clothing, are often dictated by geography and by the calendar. But whatever the local climate or time of year, iced desserts are never out of fashion. Whether the weather outside is frightful or balmy, these cooling concoctions are always welcome at the dinner table—as much so at the end of a hearty winter menu as after a light July luncheon.

There are two basic kinds of iced desserts represented by the recipes in this chapter: those that are made with milk or cream and those that usually are not. In the latter, and lighter, category are sorbets, sherbets, ices and granitas. They may differ a bit in texture—sherbets and sorbets are smoother, ices and granitas more granular and "icy"—but all are guaranteed refreshers. Most are made with fruit, from familiar varieties like strawberries, raspberries, melons, cranberries and pineapples, to more exotic specimens such as papayas, mangos and kumquats. A few *haute* versions are made with wine or brandy; and for the adventurous there is a trio of desserts based on very unusual flavorings—honey, tea, and saffron.

Ice cream needs no introduction, and certainly no defense: It is a rare guest indeed who says "no thanks" when offered a dish of this favorite. But there are many different kinds of "ice creams," and most of the examples here are not made with cream at all, but with half and half or milk—even skim milk. The result is a lighter dessert, but one that is every bit as satisfying as its heavyweight counterpart. As these recipes amply demonstrate, ice creams can be flavored with anything under the sun—berries, figs, cassis, almonds, coffee, avocado, rum, Marsala—even ginger or green tea for the perfect finish to an Oriental feast.

Colorful, tasty and very easy to prepare, iced creations such as these are often the perfect answer to the inevitable question, "What's for dessert?" One hint: To avoid being thought unfashionable, make a lot.

Sorbets, Sherbets and Ices

Raspberry-Apple Sorbet

Makes 1 quart

⅔ cup sugar
⅔ cup water
1 10-ounce package frozen raspberries, thawed, undrained

3 large tart apples (preferably Granny Smith), peeled, cored and pureed
2 tablespoons applejack

Combine sugar and water in small saucepan over medium-high heat and stir until sugar is dissolved. Just before syrup comes to boil, remove from heat. Allow to cool, then cover and chill.

Puree raspberries in processor or blender. Press through sieve to remove seeds. Add to remaining ingredients with syrup and blend well. Finish in either ice cream maker or freezer.

Cantaloupe Sorbet in Melon Cups

Can be prepared up to 2 weeks ahead. Wrap tightly in plastic when sorbet is completely frozen.

4 servings

2 cantaloupes
¾ cup water
½ cup superfine sugar

¼ cup dark rum
1 egg white
Fresh mint leaves (garnish)

Cut cantaloupes in half and remove seeds. Slice small portion off bottom of each so halves stand upright. Spoon melon pulp into processor or blender; transfer melon shells to freezer. Puree melon pulp until smooth (about 2¼ cups puree). Set aside. Combine water and sugar in small saucepan and bring to boil over medium heat, stirring until sugar is dissolved. Reduce heat; simmer 5 minutes. Remove from heat. Stir in rum. Cool.

Blend melon puree into rum mixture. Pour into shallow baking dish or ice cube tray and freeze until solid.

Remove cantaloupe mixture from freezer and let stand until slightly softened. Spoon chunks into processor or blender and mix until smooth and fluffy. Add egg white and blend until satiny. Divide mixture among melon shells, mounding as necessary. Freeze until firm, at least 3 hours. Soften at room temperature several minutes before serving. Garnish with mint.

Apricot Yogurt Ice

Makes 2 quarts

1 1-pound 14-ounce can unsweetened pitted apricots
2 packages unflavored gelatin

2 tablespoons honey
2 cups plain yogurt

2 tablespoons sugar
2 tablespoons dark rum

Fruit Sauce (see following recipe)
Toasted slivered almonds

Drain apricots, reserving liquid. Mix gelatin with ⅓ cup liquid. Bring remaining liquid to boil and pour into gelatin mixture. Stir until gelatin is completely dissolved.

Place apricots, honey, yogurt, sugar and rum in blender or processor and whirl until smooth. Stir apricot puree into gelatin mixture.

Freeze in ice cream maker according to manufacturer's instructions, or freeze in refrigerator trays, beating 2 or 3 times during freezing process. Serve with fruit sauce and sprinkling of toasted slivered almonds.

Fruit Sauce

This sauce keeps well in the refrigerator and is handy to have on hand for impromptu sundaes of all kinds.

Makes about 2 cups

1 cup dried apricots
¾ cup water

½ cup sugar
1 8½-ounce can crushed pineapple

Place apricots and water in heavy-bottomed saucepan and cook, covered, over very low heat until fruit is pulpy and falls apart when stirred. Add sugar and stir until dissolved. Add crushed pineapple with juice and bring mixture to boil. Remove from heat. Chill before serving.

Cranberry Sorbet with Kiwi

For simple sauce, reserve ¾ cup puree before freezing remainder.

6 servings

2 12-ounce packages fresh cranberries, washed
2 cups water
1½ cups sugar
¼ cup fresh orange juice
¼ cup fresh lime juice

2 tablespoons cranberry liqueur *or* kirsch

6 kiwi fruit

Combine cranberries and water in large saucepan over medium-high heat. Cover and cook until berries pop, about 3 minutes. Drain well. Transfer cranberries to blender. Add sugar, orange juice, lime juice and cranberry liqueur or kirsch and puree until smooth. Press mixture through sieve into medium bowl. Let cool. Transfer to ice cream maker and freeze according to manufacturer's instructions. Freeze at least 2 hours.

Just before serving, peel and thinly slice kiwi fruit. Overlap slices in circular pattern on individual plates, leaving open area in center. Scoop sorbet into centers and serve immediately.

Adaline's Cranberry Sherbet

Makes about 2 quarts

3 cups water
3 cups sugar
4 cups (1 quart) fresh cranberries, rinsed and drained

2 envelopes unflavored gelatin softened in 1 cup water
2 tablespoons fresh lemon juice

Combine water and sugar in 4-quart saucepan over medium-high heat. Add cranberries and cook, stirring occasionally, until berries pop and soften, about 8 minutes. Remove from heat. Stir in softened gelatin, blending well. Strain mixture into large bowl, pressing with back of wooden spoon to extract as much pulp as possible. Blend in lemon juice. Pour mixture into container and freeze overnight.

Spoon sherbet into processor or blender and mix until smooth. Return to container and freeze another 6 hours. Let soften in refrigerator about 10 minutes before serving.

Berry Sherbet

Makes about 2 cups

1½ cups unsweetened frozen
   blueberries, strawberries *or*
   raspberries, slightly thawed

½ cup sugar
1 egg white

Puree all ingredients in processor or blender until smooth. Pour into shallow pan. Cover and freeze until firm.

Grape Harvest Sorbet with Leaf Cookies

4 servings

1¼ pounds Ribier grapes, seeded
⅓ to ½ cup sugar (depending on
   sweetness of grapes)
1 tablespoon fresh lemon juice

8 large grape leaves *or* other large
   fresh leaves, washed and dried
8 Leaf Cookies (see following
   recipe)

Set dessert plates in freezer. Puree grapes with sugar and lemon juice in processor or blender. Strain through fine sieve into small bowl. Let stand at room temperature until sugar is dissolved, about 30 minutes. If ice cream maker is available, turn into machine and freeze according to manufacturer's instructions. Transfer to freezer for 2 hours. If ice cream machine is not available, pour strained puree into shallow pan and freeze until firm, about 4 hours, stirring with fork every 30 minutes at first and more frequently toward end of freezing time. Transfer to processor or blender and mix well. Refreeze until ready to form balls.

Arrange 2 leaves on each chilled plate. Working quickly with small ice cream scoop or melon baller, form "cluster" of grape sorbet balls in center of dishes. Cover with plastic and refreeze. Serve with cookie placed over each leaf.

Leaf Cookies

*Makes about 3 dozen
large cookies*

1 cup (2 sticks) unsalted butter,
   room temperature
1½ cups sifted powdered sugar
1 egg
1 teaspoon almond extract
½ teaspoon vanilla extract

2¾ cups all purpose flour
1 teaspoon baking soda
1 teaspoon baking powder

All purpose flour

Cream butter with powdered sugar in large bowl. Add egg and extracts and beat well. Blend in dry ingredients. Transfer dough to plastic bag and pat into circle ½ inch thick. Refrigerate at least 1 hour, preferably overnight, or chill in freezer for 30 minutes.

Preheat oven to 375°F. Generously grease baking sheet(s). Roll out dough on lightly floured surface to thickness of ⅛ inch. Cut out cookies from dough using large leaf-shaped cookie cutter or homemade cardboard stencil (if using stencil, trace shape with tip of small knife). Transfer cookies to baking sheet(s). Bake until lightly golden, about 10 minutes, checking to prevent overbaking. Let cool slightly, then transfer to racks and cool completely.

Citrus Fruit Sorbet with Cognac

A garnish of freshly ground pepper enhances the fresh citrus flavor.

8 servings

2 cups water
1¼ cups sugar
2 tablespoons grated lemon peel (about 3 large lemons)

¾ cup fresh lemon juice (unstrained)

½ cup fresh tangerine *or* orange juice (unstrained)

8 tablespoons Cognac
Freshly ground pepper (optional garnish)

Mix water, sugar and lemon peel. Cover and let stand at room temperature at least 4 hours or overnight.

Restir mixture to dissolve sugar as much as possible. Strain into medium bowl. Discard peel. Blend in lemon and tangerine juices. If ice cream maker is available, transfer mixture to machine and freeze according to manufacturer's instructions. Transfer sorbet to plastic container, packing tightly to prevent air pockets. Press piece of plastic wrap over sorbet. Cover and freeze up to several days. Let soften in refrigerator about 20 minutes before using. If ice cream maker is unavailable, freeze sorbet in shallow metal pan (such as ice tray) until almost solid. Break into chunks and mix in processor or blender until smooth. Refreeze until almost frozen or until ready to serve.

To serve, scoop sorbet into individual goblets. Top each portion with 1 tablespoon Cognac. Garnish with small amount of pepper if desired.

Avocado-Lime Sorbet

Hollowed-out lime halves garnished with mint are the perfect "dishes" for this sorbet, whether served as dessert or palate refresher.

Makes about 3¼ cups

⅔ cup sugar
⅔ cup water

2 large ripe avocados, peeled and pureed

¼ cup fresh lime juice
Drop of hot pepper sauce
Pinch of salt

Combine sugar and water in small saucepan over medium-high heat and stir until sugar is dissolved. Just before syrup comes to a boil, remove from heat. Cool slightly, then cover and chill.

Beat avocado with lime juice until completely smooth. Add pepper sauce and salt and blend well. Chill. Stir in syrup. Finish in ice cream maker or freezer.

Mango-Honey Ice

Makes about 3 cups

4 very ripe medium-size mangoes
½ cup water
2 tablespoons honey

2 tablespoons fresh lemon juice

Cut mangoes in half. Spoon pulp into processor or blender, scraping as much pulp away from seed as possible. Puree until smooth (about 3 cups puree). Set aside. Combine water and honey in small saucepan and bring to boil over medium heat, stirring occasionally to dissolve honey. Reduce heat and simmer 5 minutes. Remove from heat and let cool.

Blend lemon juice and honey mixture into mango puree. Pour into shallow baking dish or ice cube tray and freeze until firm, about 3 hours. Let stand at room temperature 5 to 10 minutes to soften slightly. *(If freezing for longer than 3 hours, adjust softening time as necessary.)* Spoon into bowls or wine glasses and serve.

🍎 *Frozen Fruit Desserts*

With their icy tang and cool essence of fresh fruit, frozen fruit desserts can be the perfect ending to a summer meal or a welcome interlude between courses. Despite their glamorous reputation, they are extremely simple to prepare and can be made and frozen several weeks before you intend to use them. The three types of desserts covered here—sorbets, granitas and fruit puree ices—have become the darlings of fanciers of the new, lighter cuisine because they are excellent examples of its principles: fresh ingredients treated in ways that enhance their natural flavors. The fact that they are low in calories doesn't hurt, either!

These fruit ices distinguish themselves from sherbets, ice creams and parfaits by avoiding the use of milk, eggs or cream. The smoothest, the French sorbet, is coaxed to a fine texture by the addition of egg white. One superb version is Cantaloupe Sorbet in Melon Cups (page 72) served prettily in its own frozen "shell." To ensure the silkiest possible texture, chill the processor work bowl or blender container. The granita, with its frosty unbeaten ice crystals, is one of Italy's contributions to the world of frozen desserts.

Although these recipes use the still freezing method—no special equipment is necessary—sorbets and granitas also can be made in an ice cream maker. Sorbets need a low ratio of salt to ice so they will freeze slowly and develop a velvety smoothness. Granitas, on the other hand, require a high ratio of salt to ice so they will freeze quickly and preserve their distinctive rough texture. To "ripen" desserts made in an ice cream maker, stir the mixture after it is churned and then pack into freezer containers, allowing an inch of space at the top for expansion. Cover tightly and freeze for 2 to 3 hours before serving.

The third type of recipe—fruit puree ice, such as Mango-Honey Ice (page 75)—is perhaps the easiest of all. Pureed fruit is simply mixed with a little syrup and then frozen.

When selecting fruit, choose only the ripest to be sure the flavor and sugar content are fully developed. With each recipe, taste the mixture after it

Gingered Nectarine Sorbet with Strawberries

Select only the ripest and sweetest nectarines for this smooth sorbet.

6 servings

Sorbet
½ cup dry white wine
⅓ cup sugar
1½ to 2 tablespoons minced candied ginger

4 large ripe nectarines, peeled, pitted and chopped
1 teaspoon grated lemon peel

Juice of 1 lemon

Yogurt Sauce
1 cup plain yogurt
1 tablespoon honey
⅛ teaspoon cinnamon

18 large strawberries, rinsed but not hulled

For sorbet: Combine wine, sugar and ginger in medium saucepan over medium heat and cook until sugar is dissolved. Increase heat to high and boil 5 minutes.

is blended and then adjust the sweetness to your own taste. In some cases you may want to add more sugar, and in others, where the fruit is very ripe, a squeeze of lemon juice will help strike the proper sweet–tart balance. You might want to oversweeten the mixture slightly, as freezing diminishes the intensity of both sugar and honey; however, too much sugar can inhibit freezing, so never use more than 1 part sugar for every 4 parts liquid and fruit combined. Superfine sugar, rather than regular, works best for water ices because it dissolves so easily.

To create your desserts, a good general formula is 2 cups fruit *plus* 1 to 1½ cups liquid *plus* ½ cup sugar. However, when using the best seasonal fruit, much of the liquid will be supplied by the fruit's own juice.

Using the recipes in this section as a guide, and the succulent fruits of summer for inspiration, any cook can create a veritable rainbow of fresh, cooling desserts.

Tips

- If you have no superfine sugar on hand, mix granulated sugar in processor or blender until very fine.
- Fruit desserts may crystallize after long freezer storage. Let soften slightly, then remix in processor or blender. Refreeze the dessert for several hours before serving.
- A heavy-duty mixer can be substituted for a processor or blender.
- For convenient small servings, prepare recipe as directed, freezing mixture in ice cube trays with divider in. Remove cubes and store in freezer in plastic bags. To serve, reprocess or reblend only what is needed, leaving remaining cubes in bags in freezer.

Remove from heat and let cool to room temperature. Cover and chill thoroughly. *(Syrup can be prepared several weeks ahead.)*

Combine nectarines, lemon peel and juice in processor or blender and puree. Add cold syrup and blend well. Taste and add more ginger if desired. Turn sorbet into shallow pan and freeze. Can be prepared several days ahead to this point.

For sauce: Combine yogurt, honey and cinnamon in small serving bowl and whisk until well blended.

To assemble, place 3 strawberries on each dessert plate. Cut sorbet into small squares and puree in batches in processor or blender. Shape sorbet into ovals using 2 tablespoons. Arrange 2 ovals on each plate and drizzle with strip of sauce. Serve immediately. Dip berries in remaining sauce.

Orange Alaska

4 to 6 servings

4 to 6 oranges

Orange Yogurt Sherbet
  1 cup orange sherbert, softened
  1 cup orange yogurt
  ¼ cup fresh orange juice
  ¼ cup orange liqueur
  1 teaspoon grated orange peel

Meringue
  2 egg whites
  ¼ teaspoon cream of tartar
  3 tablespoons sugar
  ¼ teaspoon vanilla

  Lemon leaves (garnish)

Cut circular section from top of each orange. Scoop out pulp, squeeze and strain, reserving juice to add to sherbet.

For sherbet: Combine orange sherbet and yogurt and stir until thoroughly blended. Add orange juice, orange liqueur and orange peel and mix well. Spoon sherbet into orange shells and place immediately in freezer.

For meringue: Whip egg whites until frothy. Add cream of tartar and continue to whip eggs until soft peaks form. Gradually add sugar and vanilla and continue beating until whites are stiff and glossy.

Spread top of each orange shell with meringue, completely covering sherbet and bringing meringue down well over edge. Place in freezer.

Just before serving, preheat broiler. Broil oranges just until meringue turns golden, not more than 3 minutes. *Watch carefully.*

Serve each Orange Alaska on bed of fresh, glossy green lemon leaves.

Papaya Sorbet in Papaya Shells

Can be prepared up to 2 weeks ahead. Wrap tightly in plastic when sorbet is firm.

8 servings

4 large papayas, halved and seeded
2 cups water
½ cup superfine sugar
¼ cup fresh lime juice

1 egg white
Halved strawberries (garnish)

Spoon papaya pulp into processor or blender; transfer papaya shells to freezer. Puree pulp until smooth (about 3 cups puree). Set aside. Combine water and sugar in medium saucepan and bring to boil over medium heat, stirring until sugar is dissolved. Reduce heat and simmer 5 minutes. Remove from heat. Let cool. Stir in fresh lime juice.

Blend papaya puree into lime mixture. Pour into shallow baking dish or ice cube tray and freeze until solid.

Remove papaya mixture from freezer and let stand until slightly softened. Spoon chunks into processor or blender and mix until smooth and fluffy. Add egg white and blend until smooth and satiny. Divide mixture among papaya shells, mounding as necessary. Freeze until firm, at least 3 hours. Soften at room temperature several minutes before serving. Arrange row of halved strawberries around top edge of each papaya half.

Ananas Givre

Fresh pineapple sorbet will bedazzle even your most discriminating guests.

6 servings

1 to 2 large fresh pineapples
Light corn syrup

1 cup plus 5 tablespoons water
1½ cups plus 1 tablespoon sugar
¼ teaspoon unflavored gelatin *or* pectin
¼ cup kirsch

Ananas Confit au Kirsch (see following recipe)

Angelica *or* mint leaves (garnish)
Maraschino cherries (optional garnish)

Remove lengthwise slice of pineapple, being careful not to disturb crown (cut surface and leaves should be level). Using a curved knife, carefully hollow out pineapple meat, making sure pineapple shell is not cut or broken. Remove and discard core. Weigh pineapple meat; you will need 2 pounds 3 ounces. If there is not enough, cut into second pineapple. Brush inside of pineapple shell with corn syrup and freeze.

Finely chop pineapple in processor or run through food grinder. Put through food mill or press through strainer to extract all juices from puree. Press third time using chinois, fine strainer or sieve. Reserve all juice and puree; discard pulp.

Bring water, sugar and gelatin to boil in small saucepan over medium-high heat, stirring only until sugar dissolves. Remove from heat and add both pineapple puree and juice. Transfer to ice cream maker and process according to manufacturer's directions, 15 to 20 minutes. Stir in kirsch. Remove almost half the mixture and place in pastry bag fitted with plain tip. Freeze.

Line frozen pineapple shell with ½ inch sorbet from ice cream maker. Dot with portion of Ananas Confit au Kirsch. Repeat layering twice more. End with final layer of sorbet level with top of pineapple shell. Top with layer of Ananas Confit au Kirsch. Using pastry bag, decorate with overlapping "fingers" of sorbet. Repeat with second shell. Dot with additional Ananas Confit and desired garnish(es). Freeze uncovered. When surface is quite firm, wrap completely in freezer paper or foil.

Fifteen minutes before serving, place in refrigerator to soften slightly. Decorate with leaves and serve with additional Ananas Confit au Kirsch.

Ananas Confit au Kirsch (Pineapple in Kirsch)

Can be stored indefinitely in refrigerator in airtight container.

Makes about 4 cups

2 cups plus 2 tablespoons water
3 cups sugar
35 ounces well-drained canned

pineapple chunks (use 2½ 1-pound 4-ounce cans)
⅓ cup kirsch

Combine water and sugar in medium saucepan and bring to boil over medium-high heat, stirring until sugar dissolves. Cook without stirring until candy thermometer registers 220°F. Add pineapple, reduce heat and simmer 1 to 2 minutes. Remove from heat and allow to cool before adding kirsch.

Pineapple-Coconut Sherbet

A refreshingly tart finish.

4 to 5 servings

2 7½-ounce cans crushed pineapple packed in its own juice
1 pint plain yogurt (not nonfat)
½ cup unsweetened shredded coconut

Toasted slivered almonds (garnish)

Combine all ingredients except garnish and blend well. Pour into shallow pan or freezer tray and freeze until mushy. Transfer to mixing bowl and beat vigorously 3 to 4 minutes. Return to pan or tray, cover and refreeze until solid.

Before serving, beat sherbet in processor or by hand until smooth. Turn into dessert dishes and return to freezer. Top with toasted almonds.

Raspberry Cassis Granita

Makes about 3 cups

2 10-ounce packages frozen raspberries in syrup, thawed
1 cup water
¼ cup superfine sugar

½ cup crème de cassis
2 tablespoons fresh lemon juice

Using back of spoon, press raspberries through fine strainer into bowl to extract as much pulp as possible. Discard seeds. Set pulp aside. Combine water and sugar in small saucepan and bring to boil over medium heat, stirring until sugar is dissolved. Reduce heat and simmer 5 minutes. Let syrup cool.

Blend cassis, lemon juice and syrup into raspberry pulp. Pour into shallow baking dish or ice cube tray and freeze until edges are solid but center is still slightly soft, about 1½ hours.

Spoon granita into processor or blender in batches and chop using on/off turns until texture is that of coarse puree. Return to shallow dish or tray and freeze. Repeat chopping and return to freezer. Chop third time, then freeze overnight before serving.

Fresh Kumquat Ice

Accompany with fortune cookies.

Makes 2 quarts

4 cups fresh kumquats
2½ cups sugar
4 cups water
3 cups fresh orange juice

6 tablespoons fresh lemon juice

Orange liqueur *or* vodka (optional)

Wash kumquats in hot water. Halve and remove seeds. Puree in processor or blender in batches using on/off turns until smooth. Turn into heavy large saucepan. Add sugar and bring to boil. Reduce heat to low and simmer 15 minutes, stirring frequently. Blend in water and juices. Cool completely. Chill several hours or overnight.

Strain kumquat mixture into ice cream maker and freeze according to manufacturer's instructions. Transfer to airtight container and freeze 3 to 4 hours. (If ice cream maker is not available, freeze mixture in shallow trays. Before serving, spoon into processor or blender in batches and mix using on/off turns until smooth. Return to freezer just until firm.) Spoon ice into individual serving dishes. Pour orange liqueur or vodka over each serving, if desired.

Tangerine Ice

Makes 1 quart

¾ cup sugar
½ cup water
3 cups fresh tangerine juice
1 to 2 tablespoons fresh lemon
  juice

Finely slivered lime peel and mint
sprigs (garnish)

Combine sugar and water in large saucepan over low heat and swirl pan gently until sugar is dissolved. Cool syrup completely. Blend in tangerine and lemon juices. Refrigerate until well chilled, at least 1 hour. If ice cream maker is available, transfer mixture to machine and process according to manufacturer's instructions. Turn into plastic container. Cover and freeze until ready to use. If ice cream maker is unavailable, freeze mixture in shallow metal trays. Break into pieces, then mix in processor until smooth. Refreeze in metal trays until firm. Store in airtight container. Let soften slightly before serving. Garnish with lime peel and mint.

Frozen Fruit Special

4 servings

1 20-ounce package frozen mixed
  fruits, thawed
¼ cup kirsch *or* Grand Marnier

1 pint rainbow, lemon *or* other
  sherbet

Fresh mint leaves (optional
garnish)

Mix fruits with liqueur. When ready to serve, place fruits in glass serving dish and top with scoops of sherbet. Garnish with mint.

Honey Ice

6 servings

1½ cups cold water
½ cup honey
1 cup fresh orange juice
2 tablespoons fresh lemon juice
1 teaspoon grated orange peel
½ teaspoon cinnamon

Pinch of salt

1 cup whipping cream
6 tablespoons Grand Marnier
3 tablespoons chopped pistachios
(garnish)

Beat water and honey in saucepan until thoroughly blended. Place over medium heat and bring to boil. Let boil 2 minutes without stirring. Remove from heat and add next 5 ingredients. Strain into ice tray or shallow dish. Freeze.

When ready to serve, whip cream. Scoop ice into bowls and pour a tablespoon of Grand Marnier over each. Top with whipped cream and pistachios.

Papaya Yogurt Ice

Makes 1 quart

2 large papayas
3 tablespoons fresh lime juice
1 teaspoon vanilla

2 eggs, separated
¾ cup sugar
Pinch of salt

2½ cups plain yogurt

Papaya halves
Burnished Coconut (see following recipe)
Lime wedges (garnish)

Peel and seed papayas and cut meat into chunks. Whirl in blender or processor until papaya is pureed (about 2 cups puree). Add lime juice and vanilla.

Combine egg yolks, ¼ cup sugar and salt. Beat with electric mixer on high speed until yolks are light and lemon colored. Stir in papaya mixture. Add ¼ cup sugar. Beat sugar into mixture until it dissolves. Stir in yogurt.

In large bowl, beat egg whites until soft peaks form. Slowly pour in remaining ¼ cup sugar and continue beating until stiff and glossy.

Fold papaya mixture into egg whites, stirring just until blended. Freeze in ice cream maker according to manufacturer's instructions, or freeze in ice cube trays, stirring occasionally during freezing process.

When mixture is frozen, spoon into fresh papaya halves, top with sprinkle of Burnished Coconut and garnish with lime wedges.

Burnished Coconut

Makes about 1 cup

1 cup moist, shredded coconut
¼ cup firmly packed brown sugar

1 tablespoon butter

Toss coconut and brown sugar together in mixing bowl. Melt butter in heavy saucepan over low heat. Add coconut and sugar mixture and cook, stirring constantly, until golden brown and sugar crystals are dissolved, 5 to 7 minutes. Cool and sprinkle over Papaya Yogurt Ice.

Saffron Sorbet

4 to 6 servings

2¼ cups water
½ cup plus 2 tablespoons sugar
Pinch of saffron threads
Strained juice of 5 medium lemons

1 teaspoon anise liqueur
4 to 5 fresh mint leaves (garnish)

Combine water and sugar in medium saucepan. Cook over low heat until sugar dissolves, swirling pan occasionally. Increase heat to medium high and bring syrup to boil. Stir in saffron. Let cool. Mix in lemon juice and liqueur. Transfer to ice cream maker and process according to manufacturer's instructions. Scoop into dessert bowls or glasses. Garnish with mint leaves.

Glace au Sauternes

2 to 4 servings

2 cups water
¾ cup sugar

½ cup Sauternes *or* other sweet dessert wine

3 to 4 tablespoons fresh lemon juice
1 teaspoon finely grated lemon peel

Combine water and sugar in heavy small saucepan. Bring to boil, stirring just until sugar dissolves. Let boil 5 minutes. Cool completely.

Stir in remaining ingredients, blending well. Pour into freezer tray and freeze until solid, stirring several times (or freeze in ice cream maker according to manufacturer's instructions). Spoon into processor or blender and mix briefly. Turn into chilled dessert dishes or goblets and serve immediately.

Russian Tea Sorbet

4 to 6 servings

4 cups freshly brewed hot black tea
¾ cup sugar
1 to 2 tablespoons Grand Marnier
2 whole cloves
1 large bay leaf

1 1-inch piece cinnamon stick
Grated peel of 1 orange
Juice of 1 lemon
Juice of 1 orange
Mint sprigs (garnish)

Pour hot tea into large bowl. Add sugar, Grand Marnier, cloves, bay leaf, cinnamon stick, orange peel, lemon juice and orange juice and mix well. Let stand at room temperature about 3 hours to steep. Strain into large bowl. If ice cream maker is available, transfer tea to machine and process according to manufacturer's instructions. If ice cream maker is unavailable, pour tea mixture into metal tray and freeze 4 hours, stirring every 20 minutes with fork to break up ice crystals that form on sides of tray. Thirty minutes before serving, mix tea in processor until creamy, then refreeze. Spoon into goblets or glass tea cups and garnish with fresh mint sprigs.

Red Wine Ice with Fresh Fruit

8 servings

4 cups Zinfandel *or* other dry red wine
2 cups water
¾ cup sugar
2 tablespoons grated lemon peel
1 1½-inch piece cinnamon stick

2 tablespoons fresh lemon juice

Ripe melon *or* pear slices, sprinkled with lemon juice (garnish)

Combine wine, water, sugar, lemon peel and cinnamon in large saucepan. Bring to boil, stirring often, until sugar dissolves. Reduce heat to medium low and simmer 5 minutes, uncovered. Cool mixture to room temperature. Stir in lemon juice. Pour mixture into 2 shallow metal pans and freeze overnight.

Several hours before serving, transfer half of ice to blender in small batches or processor and blend until smooth. Repeat with remaining ice. Return ice to freezer. Fifteen minutes before serving, transfer ice to refrigerator to soften slightly. Scoop into individual bowls and garnish with ripe melon or pear slices.

Granité au Champagne

For variation, use half Chandon Napa Valley Brut and half Chandon Blanc de Noirs.

Makes about 1 quart

1 bottle Chandon Napa Valley Brut

½ cup sugar, or to taste

1 teaspoon kirsch

Combine all ingredients quickly, blending *only until sugar is dissolved (do not overmix or wine will lose its effervescence)*. Pour into shallow pan and freeze until firm. To serve, scrape ice to form ball of desired size for individual serving.

Calvados Sherbet

4 servings

1 cup plus 1 tablespoon apple juice
⅞ cup water
½ cup sugar
1 tablespoon fresh lemon juice

1 egg white
1 tablespoon sugar
2 tablespoons Calvados

Combine apple juice, water, ½ cup sugar and lemon juice in small saucepan. Place over medium-high heat and stir until sugar is dissolved. Just before syrup reaches boiling point, remove from heat. Let stand until cool, then chill thoroughly.

Beat egg white until foamy. Add remaining 1 tablespoon sugar and beat until stiff. Add syrup and Calvados and blend well. Turn into ice cream maker and freeze according to manufacturer's instructions.

Ice Cream Bombe

6 to 8 servings

3 pints raspberry sherbet, softened
2 pints pink peppermint ice cream, softened

2 cups whipping cream
3 tablespoons powdered sugar
⅛ teaspoon salt

½ cup chopped dried apricots
½ cup slivered almonds, toasted
¼ cup chopped crystallized ginger
⅓ cup brandy, or to taste

Chill 3-quart mold and metal spatula. With chilled metal spatula, spread raspberry sherbet quickly over bottom and sides of mold to the top. Freeze until firm. Make layer of peppermint ice cream on top of raspberry sherbet. Freeze until firm.

Whip cream, gradually adding sugar and salt. When cream forms stiff peaks, fold in apricots, almonds and ginger. Add brandy. Fill cavity in mold completely with whipped cream mixture. Cover with plastic wrap and freeze.

To unmold, invert chilled platter over mold and turn right side up. Wrap hot towels around mold to loosen. Serve dessert immediately.

Fresh Strawberry Sorbet

For a pretty presentation, sorbet may be served in lemon shells. Garnish with mint leaves, if desired.

Apples, apricots, peaches, raspberries, melons and nectarines can be substituted for strawberries, always using 3 to 3½ cups of the pureed fruit.

8 servings

Peel of 1 lemon (yellow part only), finely minced
⅔ cup sugar *or* honey
⅔ cup water
¼ cup fresh lemon juice

6 cups strawberries, chopped

2 large egg whites
2 teaspoons sugar (optional)

Combine minced lemon peel, sugar and water in small saucepan and boil until sugar dissolves, about 2 minutes. (If using honey, simply combine with peel, water is not necessary, but do not heat.) Strain lemon juice and set aside.

Place strawberries in processor or blender and puree in batches. Add lemon peel mixture and lemon juice to strawberry puree and blend to combine thoroughly. Transfer to shallow container and freeze.

Meanwhile, beat egg whites with electric mixer until stiff but not dry. If using sugar, beat in remaining 2 teaspoons; omit if using honey.

Allow frozen sorbet to thaw until just softened, but not runny. Place partially thawed strawberry mixture in processor or blender by spoonfuls. Puree, using on/off turns, then let machine run until mixture is thoroughly blended and fluffy. Fold about ¼ cup into egg whites, then fold in remainder. Return to freezer until quite firm, at least 2 hours.

Ice Creams

Avocado Ice Cream

2 to 4 servings

1½ teaspoons unflavored gelatin	1 large avocado, peeled and pitted
2 tablespoons cold water	½ cup plain yogurt
½ cup whipping cream	2 tablespoons fresh lime juice
1 tablespoon sugar	2 tablespoons sugar
¼ teaspoon salt	Raspberry Sauce (optional; see
1 egg, separated	following recipe)

Sprinkle gelatin over water in small dish and let stand until softened. Meanwhile, combine cream, 1 tablespoon sugar and salt in small saucepan and cook over low heat just until bubbles form at rim. Beat egg yolk and stir into gelatin. Blend gelatin mixture into cream and let cool completely.

Puree avocado in processor or blender. Add to cream mixture with yogurt and lime juice, blending well. Beat egg white in large bowl until soft peaks form. Gradually add 2 tablespoons sugar and continue beating until stiff. Fold avocado mixture into egg white. Turn into shallow pan or ice cube tray, cover with foil and freeze until firm (for lighter texture, beat mixture in processor or electric mixer several times during freezing process). Spoon into goblets and serve with Raspberry Sauce.

Raspberry Sauce

Makes about 1 cup

1 10-ounce package frozen unsweetened raspberries, thawed	¼ cup sugar
	1 tablespoon rum

Puree all ingredients in processor or blender. Strain before using.

Fresh Blueberry Ice Cream

Makes about 1½ quarts

2 cups fresh blueberries, stemmed	2½ cups half and half *or* milk
½ cup sugar	

Combine blueberries and sugar in heavy-bottomed large skillet over low heat. Cook, stirring occasionally, until sugar dissolves and mixture simmers. Remove from heat and stir in half and half, blending well. Let mixture cool to room temperature. Refrigerate until thoroughly chilled, at least 1 hour. Transfer mixture to ice cream maker and freeze according to manufacturer's instructions. Turn into plastic container. Cover and freeze until ready to use. Let ice cream soften slightly in refrigerator before serving.

❦ Simple Frozen Parfaits

Cool desserts are delightfully refreshing finales for informal warm-weather meals. The simple frozen parfait presented here really fills the bill. Suave and elegant, it has a smooth, creamy texture that gives it star status at any table. Even the novice cook will have no trouble creating this exquisite dessert in just half an hour.

Unlike typical American parfaits with their layers of ice cream, pudding, sauce and fruit, this French formula is a combination of egg yolks, cream, sugar and a flavoring.

The parfait has only a handful of ingredients, so each must be fresh, pure and prime. The more sugar it contains, the softer and more velvety the texture and the less firm the consistency. But be careful in experimenting: Too much sugar can mask the taste.

This offering is beautiful when served in dessert dishes or goblets. For a quick frozen soufflé, divide the mixture among individual ramekins that have been fitted with buttered foil collars. It can also be molded by itself or combined with ice cream, sherbet or fruit in the covered conical French mold known as a bombe. Freeze it with cake for a baked Alaska or with meringue for a vacherin.

Basic Frozen Parfait

To stabilize the parfait base, egg yolks, sugar and liquid are beaten over simmering water until very thick. They are then removed from heat and beaten to cool, because whipped cream will lose its volume if folded into a hot mixture. These steps can all be performed using a portable electric mixer (or by hand with a whisk or rubber spatula), but off-the-heat beating will be more efficient if a heavy-duty mixer is used.

4 egg yolks, room temperature
½ cup sugar
½ cup liquid (espresso *or* fresh orange juice *or* strained berry puree)

1 cup whipping cream

1 to 2 tablespoons liqueur *or* 2 teaspoons vanilla

Whipped cream rosettes, fruits, nuts *or* sauce (optional garnishes)

Place yolks in large bowl of electric mixer. Beat in sugar 1 tablespoon at a time, blending well. Gradually beat in liquid. Fill pot large enough to hold mixing bowl with water and bring to simmer. Set bowl in pot and beat mixture over very low heat until pale yellow, triple in volume and thick, scraping down sides of bowl occasionally, about 7 to 10 minutes; *do not let mixture boil or egg yolks will curdle.*

Remove mixture from heat and continue beating until cool, about 5 to 10 minutes. Beat cream with liqueur in another bowl until soft peaks form. Gently fold whipped cream into cooled yolks in 4 additions, being careful not to deflate mixture.

Pour into mold or spoon into 1 large or 4 individual serving dishes. Cover with plastic wrap. Freeze at least 4 hours. Before serving, let soften slightly in refrigerator for about 30 to 45 minutes. Garnish parfait as desired.

Variations

Lemon Blueberry Parfait: For the liquid, use 3 to 4 tablespoons strained fresh lemon juice with enough water to measure ½ cup. Fold 1 tablespoon

The parfait is best served within a day after it is made. It will keep in the freezer for several weeks afterward, but the texture will change slightly.

2 to 4 servings (about 3¾ cups)

grated lemon peel into yolk mixture. Freeze in ring mold. To serve, fill center with blueberries. Lime can be substituted for lemon. Serve with pineapple, watermelon or sweetened strawberries.

Maple or Honey Parfait: Substitute ⅓ cup maple syrup or honey for ½ cup sugar. Use milk or orange juice for liquid. Stir ⅓ cup toasted chopped nuts into yolks before folding in whipped cream. Pecans and walnuts are particularly nice with maple syrup; pistachios, almonds and hazelnuts go well with honey. Accompany with peeled and sliced peaches, nectarines or apricots.

Chocolate Parfait: Use milk for liquid. Melt 4 ounces semisweet chocolate over low heat and stir until smooth. Gradually beat melted chocolate into mixture after it is removed from heat and continue beating until cool. Before freezing, fold in scant ⅓ cup raisins that have plumped overnight in 2 tablespoons dark rum. Garnish with grated coconut.

Pralin Parfait: Pralin is an excellent addition to a basic parfait made with milk, coffee or chocolate. To make pralin, combine ⅓ cup sugar and ¼ cup water in small saucepan. Cook over low heat until sugar dissolves, swirling pan occasionally. Increase heat and boil until sugar caramelizes, washing down any sugar crystals on sides of pan with brush dipped in cold water. Stir in ⅓ cup toasted sliced almonds. Pour out onto greased baking sheet. Cool until hardened. Transfer to processor or blender and pulverize. Reserve 2 tablespoons for garnish; stir remainder into mixture before folding in cream.

Parfait Soufflé: To mold a parfait so that it extends above the rim of the mold like a soufflé, choose a soufflé dish or other bowl that is slightly smaller in volume than the parfait mixture. A 2½- to 3-cup container is ideal for any of the preceding recipes. For the collar, cut an 8-inch-wide band of aluminum foil that is 2 inches longer than the circumference of the bowl. Fold in half lengthwise and butter generously. Wrap the band around the bowl greased side in, allowing at least 2½ inches of the collar to rise above the rim. Staple the band where it overlaps and tie a string around the bowl to secure it. Spoon parfait into dish and freeze. To serve, carefully remove string and collar.

Great Hints

- When whipping cream, the greatest volume and lightest texture are obtained by using well-chilled cream and a bowl and beater that have been chilled in the freezer for at least 45 minutes.
- If parfait crystallizes after prolonged freezer storage, restore it to the original texture by pureeing it in a processor. Refreeze until serving.
- To reduce the chance of curdling, cool parfait mixture quickly by beating over ice water after removing from heat.
- Use a metal bowl or container for quick, noncrystallizing freezing and to facilitate unmolding.
- If parfait freezes solid, soften in refrigerator for 1 to 2 hours.

Fig Ice Cream

Makes 1 quart

2 cups canned peeled Kadota figs,
   quartered, well drained
1 (scant) cup sugar

2½ cups half and half *or* milk

Fresh figs (optional garnish)

Combine figs and sugar in heavy-bottomed large skillet over low heat. Cook, stirring occasionally, until sugar dissolves and mixture simmers. Continue simmering 10 minutes, stirring occasionally. Remove from heat and stir in half and half. Let cool. Refrigerate until thoroughly chilled, about 1 hour.

Transfer mixture to ice cream maker and freeze according to manufacturer's instructions. Turn into plastic container. Cover and freeze until ready to use. Let ice cream soften slightly in refrigerator before serving. Garnish with fresh figs.

Lemon-Ginger Ice Cream

Makes about 1 quart

2¼ cups half and half
   Grated peel of 3 large lemons
¾ cup sugar
6 egg yolks, room temperature

¾ cup fresh lemon juice
½ cup finely chopped preserved
   ginger in syrup, drained

Combine half and half and lemon peel in heavy medium saucepan and bring to boil slowly over very low heat. Remove from heat, cover and set aside 10 minutes. Beat sugar with yolks in large bowl until pale yellow and mixture forms slowly dissolving ribbon when beaters are lifted. Strain half and half, discarding lemon peel. Slowly pour hot half and half over yolk mixture in thin steady stream, stirring constantly. Return mixture to saucepan. Place over low heat and cook, whisking constantly, until mixture is thick enough to coat back of wooden spoon; *do not boil or mixture will curdle* (if curdling occurs, immediately transfer mixture to blender and mix at high speed until smooth). Transfer to bowl. Set over bowl of ice water. Cool completely, covering with waxed paper to prevent skin from forming on surface.

Stir lemon juice and ginger into cooled yolk mixture. Refrigerate until thoroughly chilled, at least 1 hour. Transfer mixture to ice cream maker and freeze according to manufacturer's instructions. Turn into plastic container. Cover and freeze until ready to use. Let soften slightly before serving.

White Peach Ice Cream

Makes 1 quart

1½ pounds (about 6 medium) fresh
   peaches, peeled, pitted and
   coarsely chopped
1½ cups half and half *or* milk

½ cup sugar

1 drop almond extract

Puree peaches in processor or blender (about 2⅓ cups puree). Set aside 20 to 30 minutes. Meanwhile, combine half and half and sugar in medium saucepan over low heat. Cook, stirring occasionally, until sugar dissolves, about 1 minutes. Fold sugar mixture into puree using rubber spatula. Refrigerate until thoroughly chilled, at least 1 hour.

Transfer mixture to ice cream maker and freeze according to manufacturer's instructions, adding almond extract after 15 minutes. Turn into plastic container. Cover and freeze until ready to use. Let ice cream soften slightly in refrigerator before serving.

Hazelnut Soufflé
with Mixed Fruit Sauce

From left:
Perla Meyers's Cranberry Mousse,
Crystal Butter Cookies,
Frozen Mango Mousse

Apricot Yogurt Ice

Green Tea Ice Cream,
Almond Cookies

Alan Krosnick

Clockwise from left: Tangerine Ice,
Avocado-Lime Sorbet, Fresh Strawberry Sorbet

Fresh Blueberry Ice Cream

Peaches and Cream

A delicate ice cream mousse.

10 to 12 servings

6 to 8 ripe peaches, peeled, pitted and coarsely chopped
Grated peel and juice of 1 medium orange
Grated peel and juice of 1 lemon
3 tablespoons fresh lemon juice
1 teaspoon vanilla
½ teaspoon almond extract *or* 1 teaspoon dark rum

⅓ to ⅔ cup sugar
2½ cups Crème Fraîche (see recipe, page 38), whipped and chilled
1 large peach, peeled, cut into 12 thin wedges and sprinkled with lemon juice (garnish)

Combine first 6 ingredients and ⅓ cup sugar in processor or blender and puree, adding more sugar if desired.

Transfer puree to large bowl. Gently fold in Crème Fraîche. Freeze partially, about 1 to 2 hours. Spoon into chilled ramekins and let stand at room temperature until ice crystals melt. Garnish each serving with peach wedge.

Fresh Raspberry Ice Cream

Boysenberries can be substituted for raspberries.

Makes 1½ quarts

2 cups strained fresh raspberry puree (about 5 cups whole raspberries)

2½ tablespoons fresh lemon juice
2½ cups half and half *or* milk
1 cup sugar

Combine raspberry puree and lemon juice in large bowl. Mix half and half and sugar in another bowl, stirring to dissolve sugar. Fold sugar mixture into puree using rubber spatula; do not be concerned if mixture curdles or thickens. Refrigerate until thoroughly chilled, at least 1 hour. Transfer mixture to ice cream maker and freeze according to manufacturer's instructions. Turn into plastic container. Cover and freeze until ready to use. Let soften slightly before serving.

Cassis Ice Cream

Makes 2 quarts

4 cups half and half
1¼ cups seedless blackberry jam *or* blackberry preserves
¾ cup crème de cassis

½ cup sugar
2¼ teaspoons vanilla
Crème de cassis (garnish)
Chopped walnuts (garnish)

Combine first 5 ingredients in large bowl and whisk until thoroughly blended. Transfer to ice cream maker and freeze according to manufacturer's instructions (mixture will be soft). Freeze until ready to serve. Garnish each serving with additional crème de cassis and a sprinkling of chopped walnuts.

Instant Berry Ice Cream

This may be frozen, but the texture will not be as creamy; it is best when prepared just before serving.

6 servings

1 cup whipping cream
⅓ cup sugar

1 pound unsweetened frozen berries (strawberries, blackberries, blueberries, cherries, etc.)

Place cream and sugar in blender or processor with Steel Knife and blend until thickened. Add frozen fruit a few pieces at a time and blend until smooth. Serve immediately or freeze.

Swedish Fruit Freeze

4 servings

Juice of 2 medium oranges
Juice of 2 medium lemons
1 cup sugar

1 cup milk
1 cup whipping cream, whipped

Combine orange and lemon juices in medium bowl. Blend in sugar and milk. Fold in whipped cream. Pour into ice cube tray or plastic bowl. Cover and freeze, stirring occasionally. Spoon into goblets or bowls and serve.

Kirsch Ice Cream (Crème Glacée au Kirsch)

Makes about 1 quart

8 egg yolks, room temperature
½ cup sugar
⅔ cup cold milk
1 tablespoon vanilla
½ teaspoon ground cardamom
Pinch of salt

1 cup whipping cream
¼ cup imported Kirschwasser

3 tablespoons skinned, chopped and toasted hazelnuts

Combine yolks and sugar in heavy 2-quart saucepan and whisk until mixture forms a ribbon when whisk is lifted, about 5 to 7 minutes. Whisk in half of cold milk. Place pan over medium heat and cook until thickened, about 12 minutes, whisking constantly and gradually adding remaining milk as custard thickens (custard will resemble sabayon because of incorporation of air when whisked). Cool 1 hour. Blend in vanilla, cardamom and salt.

Whip cream to soft peaks. Blend in Kirschwasser. Gently fold cream into cooled custard. Refrigerate at least 1 hour, or overnight.

If ice cream maker is available, transfer mixture to machine and freeze according to manufacturer's instructions. Turn mixture into container with tight-fitting lid and freeze up to 2 days. If ice cream maker is unavailable, freeze mixture in shallow metal trays. Mix in blender or processor until smooth. Refreeze.

To serve, spoon 2 small scoops of ice cream into individual goblets or bowls. Sprinkle with chopped nuts.

Zabaglione Ice Cream

Makes 1 quart

1½ cups milk
2 vanilla beans, split lengthwise
3 egg yolks, room temperature
⅓ cup vanilla sugar*

Vanilla Cream
2 tablespoons sugar
1 tablespoon all purpose flour

1 egg yolk, room temperature
½ cup milk, or more
1 vanilla bean, split lengthwise
1⅓ cups whipped cream (about ⅔ cup unwhipped)

⅔ cup dry Marsala

Combine milk and vanilla beans in heavy medium saucepan and bring to boil over very low heat. Remove from heat, cover and set aside 10 minutes. Meanwhile, beat yolks with sugar in large bowl until mixture is pale yellow and forms a ribbon when beaters are lifted. Remove vanilla beans from milk. Slowly pour hot milk over yolk mixture in thin steady stream, stirring constantly. Return mixture to saucepan. Place over low heat and cook, whisking constantly, until mixture is thick enough to coat back of wooden spoon. *Do not boil or mixture will curdle;*

if curdling occurs, immediately transfer mixture to blender and mix at high speed until smooth. Strain mixture back into bowl. Set over bowl of ice water. Cool completely, stirring occasionally or covering with waxed paper to prevent skin from forming on surface. Refrigerate until well chilled, at least 1 hour.

For vanilla cream: Combine sugar, flour and egg yolk in medium bowl and whisk until smooth (add 1 to 2 tablespoons milk if necessary). Combine ½ cup milk and vanilla bean in heavy-bottomed small saucepan and slowly bring to simmer over low heat. Remove from heat and discard vanilla bean. Slowly pour hot milk over yolk mixture in thin steady stream, whisking constantly. Return mixture to saucepan. Place over low heat and cook, whisking constantly, until mixture is very thick, about 8 to 10 minutes. Transfer to bowl. Set over bowl of ice water and cool thoroughly, stirring occasionally or covering with waxed paper to prevent skin from forming on surface. Fold whipped cream into cooled milk mixture using spatula.

Fold vanilla cream into chilled yolk mixture. Refrigerate until very cold. Transfer mixture to ice cream maker and freeze according to manufacturer's instructions, adding Marsala when ice cream is almost firm. Turn into plastic container. Cover and freeze. Let ice cream soften slightly before serving.

* For vanilla sugar: Combine 2 cups sugar and 1 to 2 vanilla beans in jar or canister with tight-fitting lid and shake well. Set aside for at least 5 days to blend flavors.

Ginger Ice Cream

Can be prepared up to 3 days ahead.

Makes 2 quarts

4 cups milk
6 ¼-inch-thick slices fresh ginger, coarsely chopped
8 egg yolks

1½ cups sugar

1 cup whipping cream

Combine milk and ginger in heavy nonaluminum 2- to 3-quart saucepan over low heat and cook 5 minutes, stirring occasionally. Beat yolks with sugar in large bowl until mixture is thick and lemon colored and forms a ribbon when beaters are lifted. Increase heat and bring milk to boil. Gradually whisk hot milk into yolks. Return to saucepan and cook over low heat, stirring constantly, until mixture leaves path on back of spoon when finger is drawn across; *do not boil or custard mixture will curdle.*

Strain custard through sieve lined with several layers of moistened cheesecloth set over medium bowl. Place bowl into larger bowl filled with ice. Cool custard completely, about 30 minutes, stirring occasionally. (For best results, refrigerate custard overnight to develop flavor.)

Transfer mixture to ice cream maker and freeze according to manufacturer's instructions. When ice cream begins to thicken (after about 10 to 20 minutes), whip cream until soft peaks form and add to machine. Continue processing until almost firm, about 25 minutes. Turn into plastic container. Cover and freeze until ready to use. Let ice cream soften slightly in refrigerator before serving.

Green Tea Ice Cream

6 servings

4 cups whipping cream
2 cups milk
1½ cups raw sugar
½ teaspoon ground ginger

1 heaping teaspoon green tea, ground to powder

Combine cream, milk, sugar and ginger in large bowl. Mix until sugar dissolves.

Place ground green tea in measuring cup and add enough lukewarm water to measure ¾ cup. Mix tea and water and combine with cream mixture.

Pour into ice cube tray with dividers removed and freeze. When ice is partially frozen and slushy in the center, place in blender or processor and whirl until smooth. Return to ice cube tray and freeze again.

Frozen Sherry Cream

If you like, this dessert can be made with glacéed instead of fresh fruits.

6 servings

1 quart vanilla ice cream, softened
½ cup dry *or* medium-dry Sherry

1 cup diced mixed seasonal fruits

Combine ice cream, Sherry and fruits in blender or processor and blend quickly. Pour into ice cube tray with dividers removed and freeze until mushy. Stir well, then continue freezing until firm.

Frozen Ginger Cream

Frozen cream can be made up to 1 week ahead.

8 to 10 servings

Crust
2½ cups almond cookie crumbs (about 20 cookies)
2 tablespoons (¼ stick) butter, melted

Filling
6 egg yolks

¾ cup sugar

4 egg whites
¼ cup sugar
1 cup whipping cream
¼ cup Grand Marnier
½ cup chopped crystallized ginger

For crust: Combine cookie crumbs and butter. Reserve small amount and pat remainder on bottom and slightly up sides of 8- or 9-inch springform pan. Chill while making filling.

For filling: Beat egg yolks with ¾ cup sugar in top of double boiler over warm water until thick, about 6 to 10 minutes. Turn into large bowl and let cool 5 minutes, then beat 1 more minute.

Beat egg whites until foamy. Gradually add ¼ cup sugar and beat until stiff. Fold into yolks. Whip cream in another bowl until thickened. Add liqueur and beat until stiff. Fold into egg mixture. Spoon into pan alternately with ginger. Sprinkle with reserved crumbs and freeze until ready to serve.

The Frozen Leopard

This dessert may be served chilled instead of frozen.

10 to 12 servings

3 cups crushed macaroons
1 cup sugar
1 cup half and half

Pinch of salt
3 cups whipping cream, whipped
1 cup brandy

Combine macaroon crumbs, sugar, half and half and salt in large bowl. Fold in whipped cream. Gradually fold in brandy. Spoon into individual dishes and place in freezer. Remove from freezer about 15 minutes before serving.

Toasted Almond-Snow Ice Cream in Pineapple Boats

The ice cream has a texture similar to a granita. Prepare it just before serving.

10 servings

2 large fresh pineapples (with tops), halved lengthwise

Choose 1 of the following:
4 cups strawberries, stemmed and halved
1½ pounds grapes (combination of purple and green), halved and seeded
2 cups kumquats
4 apples (combination of red and green), thinly sliced (do not peel)
3 bananas, peeled, thinly sliced and sprinkled with fresh lemon juice
3 pears, thinly sliced (do not peel)

Toasted Almond-Snow Ice Cream
1½ cups whipping cream
1½ cups sifted powdered sugar
1 tablespoon plus ¾ teaspoon vanilla extract
¼ teaspoon almond extract
8 cups (about) fresh, clean snow *or* finely crushed ice
¾ cup slivered almonds, toasted and cooled (3½ ounces)

¾ cup fresh orange juice
¼ cup kirsch

Using curved serrated knife, hollow out pineapple halves, leaving ½-inch shell (reserve shells and all juice). Discard core. Cut pineapple into ¼-inch cubes. Transfer to large bowl. Add desired fruit and toss lightly. Cover fruit and refrigerate at least 2 hours.

For ice cream: Blend cream, powdered sugar and extracts in large bowl. Gradually fold in snow until mixture is consistency of ice cream. Fold in nuts.

Add reserved pineapple juice to fruit. Blend in orange juice and kirsch. Spoon fruit into pineapple shells. Top with ice cream. Serve immediately.

Florentine Frozen Cream with Fruit

10 to 12 servings

4 egg yolks

1 cup sugar
¼ cup water

3 cups ground toasted almonds
3 to 4 tablespoons Galliano

1½ cups whipping cream
½ cup Galliano

Fresh strawberries, sliced papaya, golden raisins, figs (*or* prunes) and sliced almonds (garnishes)

Beat yolks with electric mixer until thick and pale, about 5 minutes.

Meanwhile, combine sugar and water in 1-quart saucepan over low heat and stir until dissolved. Increase heat and cook until syrup reaches soft ball stage (235°F to 240°F on candy thermometer). Gradually beat syrup into yolks and continue beating until thick and fluffy, about 15 minutes. Cool in refrigerator.

Moisten almonds with enough liqueur to bind. Press evenly onto bottom and sides of 8- or 9-inch springform pan.

Whip cream until soft peaks form. Fold into yolk mixture with ½ cup liqueur. Pour into springform pan. Freeze until firm, about 6 hours or overnight.

Let dessert stand at room temperature for 15 minutes before serving. Carefully remove springform. Cut frozen cream into wedges. Garnish each serving with fruit and almonds.

Avocado Yogurt Breeze

When the main course is something spicy, such as Mexican food or a curry, this interesting dessert departure is a subtle palate cooler.

Makes about 1 quart

1 cup whipping cream
2 tablespoons sugar
½ teaspoon salt

1 package unflavored gelatin
¼ cup cold water
2 eggs, separated

2 large ripe avocados

1 cup plain yogurt
3 tablespoons fresh lime juice
¼ cup sugar
Cold Orange Sauce (see following recipe)
Pistachios, chopped

Combine cream, sugar and salt in saucepan. Heat to just below boiling.

Soften gelatin in water and add to hot cream mixture. Beat egg yolks and stir into mixture. Cool.

Puree avocado in blender or processor. Beat avocado, yogurt and lime juice into cool cream mixture. Beat egg whites in separate bowl until soft peaks form. Gradually add ¼ cup sugar to egg whites and continue beating until stiff. Gently fold avocado mixture into egg whites. Freeze in an ice cream maker according to manufacturer's instructions, or freeze in ice cube trays, beating 2 or 3 times during freezing process. Serve plain or cloaked with Cold Orange Sauce and sprinkling of chopped pistachio nuts.

Cold Orange Sauce

This sauce may be made ahead of time and refrigerated. It is delicious spooned over any fresh fruit.

Makes about 1 cup

4 egg yolks
¾ cup sugar

¼ cup orange liqueur
½ cup whipping cream, whipped

Combine egg yolks, sugar and orange liqueur in top of double boiler and heat over hot, not boiling, water. Continue cooking, beating with whisk, until sauce is thick. Place double boiler top in pan of cracked ice and beat until sauce is cold. Fold in whipped cream.

Whipped Banana Yogurt

8 servings

⅔ cup sugar
½ cup fresh *or* frozen orange juice
Peel of 1 orange, grated

4 large bananas, cut into 1-inch pieces
2 teaspoons fresh lemon juice

1 cup plain yogurt

2 egg whites

Almond Cookies (see recipe, page 108)

Combine sugar, orange juice and peel in small saucepan over medium heat and cook until sugar is dissolved, stirring frequently. Let cool, then refrigerate.

Combine bananas and lemon juice in processor or blender and puree, stopping machine once to scrape down sides of container (you should have 2 cups puree). Add chilled syrup and blend thoroughly. Add yogurt and combine using on/off turns just until mixed; *do not overbeat*. Transfer to 8-inch round cake pan and freeze until firm.

Remove from freezer and let mixture soften slightly, just until it can easily be spooned out. Transfer to processor or blender in batches and mix until smooth and fluffy, stopping machine once to scrape down sides of container, about 2 minutes. With machine running add egg whites and mix thoroughly, about 1 minute. Return to cake pan and freeze.

Remove from freezer about 15 to 25 minutes before serving (depending on kitchen temperature) and allow to soften slightly. Turn into processor or blender in batches and mix until soft, light and uniformly smooth, about 2 minutes. Spoon into individual dishes and serve immediately with Almond Cookies.

Frozen Rum Cream with Amaretti

2 servings

2 eggs
Pinch of salt

½ cup sugar
¼ cup water
1 4-inch-long piece vanilla bean, split and seeded

3 tablespoons dark rum
1 teaspoon fresh lemon juice
1 cup crushed amaretti cookies *or* macaroons
1 cup whipping cream, whipped

Beat eggs and salt in large bowl of electric mixer until lemon colored.

Stir sugar, water and vanilla bean in heavy small saucepan over low heat until sugar dissolves. Increase heat to high and boil without stirring until syrup reaches 235°F on candy thermometer (soft ball stage), 7 minutes.

Discard vanilla bean. Gradually add syrup to eggs in slow steady stream, beating constantly. Transfer to heavy large nonaluminum saucepan and stir over medium-low heat until thick, about 5 minutes. Set pan into bowl of ice water and stir until cool. Gradually blend in rum and lemon juice. Mix in all but 2 tablespoons crushed amaretti cookies. Fold in whipped cream. Spoon mixture into two 12-ounce freezer-safe balloon glasses or dessert dishes. Sprinkle with remaining cookies. Freeze at least 4 hours.

Frozen Coffee Cream

6 servings

8 egg yolks, room temperature
¼ cup sugar
¼ cup water

½ cup coffee liqueur
1 cup whipping cream
½ cup chopped pecans

Beat egg yolks in large bowl of electric mixer until lemon colored and tripled in volume, about 10 minutes. Meanwhile, combine sugar and water in small saucepan and cook over low heat, stirring just until sugar is dissolved. Increase heat to medium, bring to boil and let boil 5 minutes without stirring. With mixer running, pour syrup into egg yolks in thin steady stream and continue beating until cold. Stir in liqueur. Whip cream in chilled bowl until soft peaks form. Gently fold cream and pecans into yolk mixture. Spoon into custard cups and freeze overnight.

5 ❦ Cookies

For many dessert lovers, cookies have a lot of built-in drawbacks. They are not big. They are not spectacular. They are not usually very rich, and are often not especially colorful. Nor do they offer much of a challenge: No matter how many you bake, they will not convince your friends that you should be the next pastry chef at the Plaza Athenée in Paris.

Turn all of this around, however, and cookies magically become a great dessert. They are small enough that you can enjoy several—even several varieties—without feeling guilty or shopping for a new wardrobe. They are indeed light, a blessing after a big meal. They are, to be sure, extremely easy, even for the novice cook, and most can be made days or weeks ahead. Cookies are wonderful in the cookie jar, unquestionably; but they can also star on the dessert tray.

The cookies in this collection come in all shapes and flavors and are decidedly international in character. From France there are *langues des chats,* sable cookies and lacy *tuiles* in several versions. From Italy there are *ancini,* delicate *pizzelle,* Sherry-laced "sack" wafers and crunchy filbert cookies. There are Albert wafers and festive *springerle* from Germany, butter cookies from Holland and the famous—and irresistible—Mexican wedding cookies. Britain and America are well represented as well, and there are even brandy snaps from Down Under.

Any of these cookies can be teamed with one of the fruit or iced desserts in previous chapters for a more elaborate presentation. But all you really need is good coffee and perhaps a selection of brandies and liqueurs to turn cookies into a splendid party dessert—one that guests never seem to tire of.

🍒 *Liqueurs: A Spirited Alternative to Dessert*

When even the lightest dessert seems too heavy, a small glass of liqueur may be the ideal way to end a meal.

Liqueurs, also known as cordials, are sweetened spirits, vibrantly flavored with fruits, nuts, seeds, flowers, herbs or spices, and often vividly colored. Along with after-dinner spirits such as brandy and fruit *eaux-de-vie,* they are classed by the French term *digestifs,* aids to the digestion—more a matter of culinary lore than medical fact. Nevertheless, they *are* drinks to relax with and savor, drinks that enliven the spirit and lighten the palette. And, at less than 200 calories for the average 1½–2-ounce glass, liqueurs are definitely lighter than many desserts.

There are literally hundreds of different liqueurs available, in myriad flavors and combinations of flavors. The brief list that follows, organized alphabetically by predominant flavor, just begins to suggest the possibilities. When reviewing it, bear in mind that two liqueurs of the same basic flavor will probably taste noticeably different, each a product of unique formulas and techniques that are closely guarded by their manufacturers. (*Note:* Generic names for liqueurs available from many manufacturers appear in lower case; specific brand names of note are capitalized.)

- **Anise Seed** (licorice flavor): anesone; anisette; ouzo; pastis; Pernod; Ricard.
- **Apricot:** Abricotine; Apry; many generic varieties.
- **Apricot Kernels** (bitter almond flavor): amaretto, available in many generic varieties; often combined with other flavors such as chocolate, coconut and coffee.

Dutch Butter Cookies with Ginger

Crystallized ginger may be used in place of preserved ginger, but flavor is not quite as delicate.

Makes 7 to 8 dozen

1 cup all purpose flour
½ cup (1 stick) butter, room temperature
½ cup sugar
1½ tablespoons water
1 teaspoon vanilla

Pinch of salt

1 to 2 egg yolks lightly beaten with few drops water
Preserved ginger *or* ginger marmalade

Place first 6 ingredients in processor and mix with on/off turns until well blended or blend with electric mixer. Form dough into long thin roll on lightly floured board, adding a little flour if mixture seems too moist. Cover and refrigerate for 1 to 2 hours.

Preheat oven to 400°F. Slice dough into rounds about the thickness of a quarter. Place on ungreased baking sheet and brush each with a little yolk mixture. Top with small piece of ginger or drop of marmalade. Bake until golden brown and holes appear on top, 4 to 5 minutes. Cool completely before removing from baking sheet.

- **Blackberry**: many generic varieties.
- **Black Currant**: crème de cassis.
- **Caraway Seed**: kümmel.
- **Cherry**: Cherristock; Cherry Marnier; maraschino; Peter Heering; many generic varieties.
- **Chocolate**: Cheri-Suisse (cherry-flavored); Choclair (coconut-flavored); crème de cacao; Sabra (orange-flavored); Vandermint (mint-flavored).
- **Coffee**: crème de cafe; crème de mocha; Gallwey's Irish Coffee (with Irish whiskey); Kahlua; Tia Maria.
- **Hazelnut**: Frangelico.
- **Herbs and Spices**: the oldest variety of liqueurs, these complex blends of flavors were originally concocted for medicinal purposes as long ago as the 16th century. Some noteworthy examples: Bénédictine (sweet and aromatic); Chartreuse (pungent and herbal); Galliano (syrupy, vanilla flavor); goldwasser (caraway and citrus, with flakes of real gold leaf); Strega (citrus flavor, strongly pungent).
- **Mint**: crème de menthe; peppermint schnapps.
- **Orange**: Aurum; Cointreau; curaçao; Grand Marnier; triple sec.
- **Raspberry**: Chambord Royale; many generic varieties.

Langues des Chats

Makes about 60 cookies

½ cup (1 stick) unsalted butter, room temperature
½ cup sugar
1 teaspoon vanilla

Pinch of salt
2 egg whites
1 cup unbleached all purpose flour, sifted

Preheat oven to 400°F. Lightly butter baking sheet. Dust with flour, shaking off excess. Set aside.

Cream butter and sugar in large bowl until light and fluffy. Add vanilla and salt and beat well. Beat in egg whites one at a time. Mix in flour.

Spoon mixture into pastry bag fitted with ½-inch plain tip. Holding bag straight up, pipe flat strips onto sheet in 3-inch lengths, spacing 1 inch apart. Bake until edges of cookies are lightly browned, about 5 to 8 minutes.

Crystal Butter Cookies

Makes about 5 dozen

¾ cup (1½ sticks) butter, room temperature
½ cup (scant) sugar
½ teaspoon vanilla
1¾ cups all purpose flour

Pinch of salt
1 egg yolk
2 cups coarsely crumbled rock candy

Line baking sheets with parchment paper. Beat together butter, sugar and vanilla on low speed of electric mixer. Add flour and salt all at once and continue beating until well blended, about 2 minutes. Wrap dough and refrigerate 30 minutes.

Preheat oven to 400°F. Divide dough into 3 equal portions. Roll each into cylinder about 1¼ inches in diameter. Refrigerate for 15 minutes.

Beat egg yolk. Roll cylinders in yolk and then into candy, pressing lightly so candy adheres to dough. Cut into slices ½ inch thick. Bake until set and lightly golden, about 12 minutes.

Chocolate Mint Chip Meringue Kisses

Makes about 65

3 egg whites, room temperature
1 teaspoon distilled white vinegar
1 cup sugar
2 to 3 drops green food coloring (optional)

1 12-ounce package mint-flavored chocolate chips

Preheat oven to 350°F. Line 2 baking sheets with double thickness of waxed paper. Beat egg whites and vinegar in large bowl of electric mixer until soft peaks form. Add sugar 1 tablespoon at a time and continue beating until stiff but not dry. Tint mixture with food coloring, if desired, until pale green. Fold in chocolate chips. Drop mixture by heaping teaspoons onto prepared baking sheets. Transfer to preheated oven and *immediately turn off*. Let meringues dry in oven at least 6 hours or overnight.

Carefully remove meringues from waxed paper. Store in airtight container in cool dry place.

Painted Sugar Cookies

Store these cookies in a tin or plastic box with waxed paper between layers for protection. Cookies may also be baked and frozen in advance; let them stand at room temperature to thaw.

Makes about 3 dozen

1 cup (2 sticks) butter, room temperature
1½ cups powdered sugar
1 egg
1 teaspoon vanilla extract
½ teaspoon almond extract

2½ cups all purpose flour
1 teaspoon baking soda

1 teaspoon cream of tartar
Cookie Paint
1 (4-ounce) can evaporated milk
Liquid or paste food coloring

Additional all purpose flour

Cream butter in medium bowl with electric mixer. Add sugar and beat well. Thoroughly blend in egg, then add vanilla and almond extracts.

Mix together flour, baking soda and cream of tartar in small bowl, then beat into creamed butter mixture and blend well. Form dough into ball and wrap in plastic wrap. Chill in refrigerator about 3 hours or until dough is firm enough to roll easily.

For paint: Pour 1 tablespoon evaporated milk into each of several small bowls or into sections of muffin tin. Tint each with different color of liquid or paste food coloring (paste will give more vibrant color).

Preheat oven to 375°F. Lightly grease several baking sheets. Arrange cooling racks on counter. Divide chilled dough into thirds and work with 1 section at a time, leaving remainder wrapped in refrigerator. Lightly flour counter or board and rolling pin. Roll out dough about ¼ inch thick, then cut into shapes with cookie cutters of your choice.

Using spatula or metal pancake turner, carefully lift cookies and place on prepared baking sheets. Using brush, paint bright designs on unbaked cookies with milk and food coloring mixtures. Place baking sheets in refrigerator a few minutes to make cookies firm. Bake in preheated oven until cookies are very lightly browned, about 7 to 8 minutes. Using spatula, transfer baked cookies to racks to become crisp. Let cool completely.

Crisp Chocolate Wafers

Makes about 4 dozen

2 tablespoons (¼ stick) butter, room temperature
2 ounces unsweetened baking chocolate, grated
⅔ cup firmly packed light brown sugar

3 egg whites, unbeaten
1 teaspoon vanilla
1 teaspoon dark rum
¼ cup plus 1 tablespoon cake flour
½ teaspoon baking powder
⅛ teaspoon salt

Lightly butter or grease cookie sheets. Preheat oven to 400°F.

Cream butter in medium bowl of electric mixer. Add chocolate and sugar and blend thoroughly. Add egg whites, vanilla and rum and beat well. Add dry ingredients and mix just until flour barely disappears; *do not overbeat.*

Drop dough by exact teaspoonfuls onto prepared cookie sheets, leaving 1 inch space between to allow for spreading. Bake 7 to 8 minutes, or until crisp. Remove immediately from sheets and transfer to racks to cool. (If the cookies become soft, place in single layer on cookie sheet and recrisp in 350°F oven about 8 to 10 minutes.)

Almond Meringues with Pine Nuts (Pinocchiate)

Makes about 2 dozen

8 ounces (about 1½ cups) slivered blanched almonds

2 egg whites, room temperature
⅛ teaspoon salt

¾ cup powdered sugar
¼ cup granulated sugar
¼ teaspoon almond extract
1 cup pine nuts

Preheat oven to 350°F. Toast almonds on baking sheet until lightly browned around edges, about 10 minutes, stirring occasionally for even browning. Let cool. Grind to dry meal. Retain oven temperature at 350°F.

Butter and flour large baking sheet, shaking off excess flour. Beat egg whites and salt in large bowl until soft peaks form. Mix sugars thoroughly in small bowl. Add sugars to whites about 1 tablespoon at a time, beating constantly until stiff. Blend in almond extract. Gently fold in ground almonds. Drop almond meringue onto prepared baking sheet by heaping tablespoons, spacing about 1 inch apart. Sprinkle tops evenly with pine nuts. Bake until lightly browned, about 15 minutes. Cool on rack.

Sundowners

For a refreshing light dessert, accompany these cookies with guava shells filled with fresh strawberries.

Makes about 3 dozen

2 cups sifted all purpose flour
1 cup firmly packed brown sugar
¼ teaspoon freshly grated nutmeg
⅛ teaspoon cinnamon
¾ cup (1½ sticks) butter, room temperature

1 egg, lightly beaten
1 tablespoon milk
2 tablespoons sugar
1¼ teaspoons cinnamon

Preheat oven to 400°F. Lightly grease baking sheet. Sift flour, brown sugar, nutmeg and ⅛ teaspoon cinnamon into large bowl. Cut in butter using pastry blender or 2 knives until mixture resembles coarse meal. Add egg and milk and mix well to form thick dough. Roll dough into 1-inch balls. Transfer to prepared baking sheet, spacing about 2 inches apart. Cover bottom of drinking glass with moistened cheesecloth or towel. Flatten cookies to thickness of ⅛ inch. Combine sugar and remaining cinnamon and stir to blend. Sprinkle sugar mixture over cookies. Bake until lightly browned around edges, about 7 to 8 minutes. Let cookies cool slightly on wire rack before serving.

Albert Wafers

Store these wafers in airtight container up to 3 weeks or freeze up to 2 months.

Makes about 5 dozen

1⅔ cups plus 1 tablespoon all purpose flour
1½ teaspoons baking powder
½ teaspoon salt
½ cup (1 stick) unsalted butter, room temperature

⅔ cup (scant) sugar
1 medium egg
¾ teaspoon vanilla
⅛ to ¼ teaspoon grated fresh lemon peel

Sift flour, baking powder and salt; set aside. Cream butter in medium bowl of electric mixer at medium speed. Add sugar and beat until light and fluffy. Beat in egg, vanilla and lemon peel. Gradually blend in sifted dry ingredients, stirring in last ½ cup by hand if mixer begins to slow down. Divide dough in half. Wrap in plastic and flatten into disc. Refrigerate at least 3 hours or preferably overnight.

Preheat oven to 375°F. Lightly grease baking sheets. Dust work surface generously with flour. Working quickly so dough stays chilled, roll dough out ⅛ inch thick, lifting frequently and dusting with flour as necessary to prevent sticking. (Dough can also be rolled out between sheets of plastic wrap or waxed paper.) Using 1¾-inch (or slightly larger) round cutter, cut out wafers one at a time. Immediately arrange on prepared baking sheets, spacing ¾ inch apart. Form dough trimmings into ball and chill thoroughly before rerolling. Using fork, prick each wafer 4 to 5 times in attractive pattern, lightly flouring fork occasionally. Bake until edges are lightly browned, about 7 to 8 minutes. Let cool several minutes, then transfer wafers to racks to cool completely.

Springerle

These cookies are enjoyable as much for their visual appeal as for their taste. In some German households, they are given as Christmas cards.

Store cookies in airtight container for up to 3 weeks; do not freeze. Sprinkle an additional tablespoon of aniseed into storage container if richer anise flavor is desired.

Makes about 3½ dozen

4 tablespoons aniseed
2 medium eggs
1 cup sugar
  Finely grated peel of 1 large lemon
¾ teaspoon vanilla extract

2 drops lemon extract
2¾ cups all purpose flour, or more

Assorted food colorings (optional)

Lightly grease 2 baking sheets; sprinkle each evenly with 2 tablespoons aniseed. Lay sheet of waxed paper on work surface and flour lightly. Dust Springerle rolling pin or cookie molds with flour. Beat eggs in medium bowl of electric mixer at medium speed until thickened and very light. Gradually add sugar, lemon peel and extracts and beat until mixture forms a ribbon when beaters are lifted, about 4 to 5 minutes. Reduce mixer speed to low and blend in 2 cups flour ½ cup at a time. Mix in remaining ¾ cup flour by hand. If necessary, knead in 2 to 3 tablespoons more flour until dough is cohesive and fairly firm. Knead dough in bowl 5 minutes. Divide in half. Wrap 1 half in plastic.

Working quickly to keep dough from drying, roll remaining half of dough out on floured waxed paper to thickness of ¼ inch. Firmly roll or press Springerle pin or molds into dough to imprint designs. Cut designs apart using pastry wheel or knife. Arrange cookies on prepared baking sheets. (Briefly knead dough trimmings and reroll; if dough seems too dry, dampen hands slightly before kneading.) Repeat rolling and cutting with remainder of dough. Let cookies stand uncovered at room temperature to dry for at least 12 hours or preferably 24.

Preheat oven to 250°F. Bake Springerle until nearly firm but not colored, about 25 minutes. Cool on racks 4 hours. If desired, dilute food colorings with water and apply light wash of color on raised areas of design; let stand until completely dry, about 1 hour.

Sables

Store Sables in airtight container in cool, dark place.

Makes 4 to 5 dozen

1¼ cups whole wheat pastry flour
¼ cup (½ stick) unsalted butter
Grated peel of 1 lemon
1½ egg yolks

2 tablespoons light honey

1 egg beaten with 1 teaspoon water (egg wash)

Combine flour, butter and lemon peel in processor and blend using on/off turns until mixture resembles coarse meal or blend with electric mixer. Combine egg yolks and honey in small bowl. Add to flour mixture and blend until combined but still crumbly. Gather dough into ball.

Preheat oven to 350°F. Cut two 24-inch sheets of waxed paper. Dust 1 sheet with flour. Place dough on top and dust with more flour. Cover dough with remaining sheet of waxed paper. Roll dough out to thickness of ¼ inch. Remove top sheet of waxed paper. Cut dough into rounds using 1-inch cookie cutter. Repeat rolling and cutting procedure with excess dough.

Transfer cookies to ungreased baking sheet. Make crisscross pattern atop each cookie using back of small sharp knife. Brush tops with egg wash to glaze. Bake 15 to 20 minutes. Cool on wire rack.

Pinwheels

Makes 3 to 4 dozen

1 recipe Sable dough (see recipe, this page)

Carob Dough
1¼ cups whole wheat pastry flour
2 tablespoons carob powder
½ teaspoon cinnamon
¼ cup (½ stick) unsalted butter

1½ egg yolks

2 tablespoons light honey
1 teaspoon vanilla

1 egg yolk beaten with 1 teaspoon water (egg wash)

Roll Sable dough out between 2 sheets of floured waxed paper into rectangle about 9 × 12 inches. Remove top paper.

For carob dough: Combine flour, carob powder and cinnamon in processor or medium bowl of electric mixer. Add butter and blend until mixture resembles coarse meal. Mix egg yolks, honey and vanilla in small bowl. Add to flour mixture and blend until combined but still crumbly. Gather dough into ball. Roll carob dough out between 2 sheets of floured waxed paper into rectangle about 9 × 12 inches. Remove paper. Brush top of Sable dough with egg wash. Set carob dough on top, lining up edges and trimming as necessary. Roll up tightly lengthwise as for jelly roll. Wrap roll in waxed paper and chill or freeze until firm.

Preheat oven to 350°F. Cut roll into slices ¼ inch thick. Arrange on ungreased baking sheet. Bake 15 to 20 minutes. Cool on wire rack.

Ancini

Makes about 30 cookies

½ cup (1 stick) butter, room temperature
1 cup sugar
3 eggs
2 teaspoons anise extract

3 cups unbleached all purpose flour
2 teaspoons baking powder
½ teaspoon salt

Preheat oven to 375°F. Grease 2 baking sheets. Cream butter with sugar in large bowl of electric mixer until light and fluffy. Add eggs 1 at a time, beating well after each addition. Beat in anise extract. In another large bowl, combine flour, baking powder and salt and toss with fork to blend. Add to anise mixture and stir through.

Turn dough out onto lightly floured surface. Divide in half. Shape each half into flat loaf about ½ inch thick, 3 to 4 inches wide and 10 inches long.

Transfer loaves to prepared baking sheets. Bake until golden, about 15 to 18 minutes. Let cool slightly. Cut loaves crosswise into 1-inch slices. Arrange slices on sides on baking sheets and continue baking until golden brown, about 3 to 6 minutes. Transfer to wire rack and let cool before serving.

Wedding Cookies

These beloved Mexican sweets can be made one day ahead.

Makes about 1 dozen

½ cup (1 stick) unsalted butter, room temperature
1 cup all purpose flour
¼ cup sifted powdered sugar
½ cup finely chopped pecans *or* finely chopped almonds, toasted

½ teaspoon vanilla
Pinch of salt

Powdered sugar

Position rack in center of oven and preheat to 350°F. Beat butter until light and fluffy. Add flour, ¼ cup powdered sugar, nuts, vanilla and salt and continue beating until mixture forms soft dough. Wrap tightly and freeze 1 hour, or refrigerate overnight until dough is firm enough to pinch off in pieces about the size of large walnuts.

Roll walnut-size pieces of dough between palms of hands into balls or half-moon shapes. Space about 1½ inches apart on ungreased baking sheet. Bake until cookies are pale golden, about 20 minutes. Cool slightly on wire racks. Dust generously with powdered sugar while still warm.

Pizzelle

Pizzelle can be stored up to 3 months in airtight tins in a cool, dark place.

Makes about 60 cookies

6 eggs
1½ cups sugar
1 cup (2 sticks) butter, melted and cooled

½ cup anise liqueur
2 tablespoons vanilla
3½ cups all purpose flour
4 teaspoons baking powder

Beat eggs in large mixing bowl. Gradually add sugar, mixing until smooth. Stir in melted butter, liqueur and vanilla. Sift flour and baking powder into another large bowl. Add to egg mixture, blending with wooden spoon until smooth (dough will be sticky).

Heat pizzelle iron over medium-high heat. Open iron and place 1 tablespoon batter in center. Close iron, squeezing handles together. When mixture stops sizzling, turn iron over and continue cooking until both sides of cookie are golden, checking frequently and turning iron as necessary, about 30 seconds on each side. Transfer pizzelle to wire rack using spatula. Repeat with remaining batter. Let cool completely.

For variations, add 1 cup very finely chopped walnuts or pecans to batter.

For chocolate pizzelle: Sift ½ cup unsweetened cocoa powder, ½ cup sugar and additional ½ teaspoon baking powder with flour and baking powder and add to egg mixture, blending well.

Vanilla Almond Crescents

Makes about 3 dozen

¼ cup plus 1 tablespoon unsalted butter, room temperature
1½ tablespoons light honey
¼ cup blanched almonds, pulverized

1 cup sifted whole wheat pastry flour
1 teaspoon vanilla

Preheat oven to 300°F. Beat butter in large bowl of electric mixer until light and creamy. Add honey and mix well. Add almonds and beat again. Stir in flour and vanilla with wooden spoon.

Lightly flour baking sheet. Roll small handful of dough between palms to form short cylinder. Transfer to work surface and use palm to roll into longer cylinder about ⅜ inch thick. Cut into 2-inch pieces. Transfer to prepared baking sheet. Bend ends of pieces to form crescents or half-moons. Repeat with remaining dough. Bake 20 to 25 minutes. Cool on wire rack.

Almond Spritz Cookies

Makes 5 to 6 dozen

1 cup (2 sticks) unsalted butter, room temperature
½ cup plus 2 tablespoons superfine sugar
3 ounces imported almond paste*
1 large egg, beaten
2 cups all purpose flour

1 teaspoon vanilla extract
1 teaspoon almond extract
Dash of salt

Sliced cherries, finely chopped nuts, sugar sprinkles (garnish)

Preheat oven to 375°F. Cream butter until light and fluffy. Add sugar, almond paste and egg. Beat thoroughly. Add flour gradually, then extracts and salt, blending completely.

Put through cookie press or in pastry bag fitted with a #5 star tube and squeeze cookies in desired *S* or other shapes onto ungreased cookie sheet. *(When not working with dough, keep remainder in refrigerator between batches.)* Decorate as desired with sliced cherries, nuts or sugar sprinkles. Bake until edges of cookies are slightly golden, 8 to 12 minutes. Remove to rack to cool.

*Imported almond paste has less sugar than the domestic variety and therefore makes a better cookie.

🍎 Coffee and . . .

For many of us, dessert isn't dessert without a cup of coffee. For some, coffee alone is dessert enough; add a light cookie or two and the meal ends with smiles and satisfaction.

A world of delightful variety awaits the coffee lover. Depending on the location it is grown in and the species of plant, as well as how the beans are harvested, dried and roasted—and, of course, brewed—coffee's flavor can vary from mellow and aromatic to strongly assertive to rich and almost chocolate-like. Some of the world's major coffee-growing regions and the general characteristics of their coffees are listed below; use it as a guide to begin your own explorations at a local coffee store.

- **Angola.** Robust; strong flavor.
- **Brazil.** Used mostly for blending. Best is Bourbon Santos, smooth, sweet, medium-bodied, with a high acidity when aged.
- **Colombia.** Full body, rich flavor and balanced acidity. Best is Medellín.
- **Costa Rica.** Full-bodied, rich and aromatic, with good acidity.
- **Dominican Republic.** Known as Santo Domingos. Well flavored and sweet, with good body.
- **Ecuador.** Usually used for blending. Sharp flavor with not much body.
- **El Salvador.** Good in blends. Smooth, good body and acidity, but not very well flavored.
- **Ethiopia.** A rich flavor almost reminiscent of wine. Sharp and pungent. Best known is Harrar.
- **Guatemala.** Flavorful and tangy, with full body and good aroma. Best are Antigua and Coban.
- **Haiti.** Mellow, sweet and mild, with medium body and acidity.
- **Hawaii.** Known as Kona. Flavorful, medium body, with slightly nutty taste.
- **India.** Low acidity, good body and light flavor. Mysore is most well known.
- **Indonesia.** Home of Java, heavy-bodied and very rich. Coffees of Sumatra and Celebes are also good.
- **Jamaica.** Known for Blue Mountain, one of the most mellow, rich, aromatic and sweet coffees of the world.
- **Kenya.** Full-bodied, sharp and slightly winey.
- **Mexico.** Sharp and aromatic. Best are Coatepec, Oaxaca and Pluma.
- **Nicaragua.** Good body, with a bitey acidity.
- **Peru.** Good body and acidity, with a slight sweetness. Best is Chanchamayo.
- **Puerto Rico.** Rich, full-bodied and sweet.
- **Tanzania.** Rich flavor, good body and sharp acidity.
- **Venezuela.** Low acidity, good body and mild flavor.
- **Yemen.** Home of Mocha, a rich, almost chocolate-flavored coffee. Often blended with Java.

Almond Cookies

Makes about 80 cookies

½ cup blanched almond pieces, lightly toasted and finely chopped
2 cups unbleached all purpose flour
1¼ teaspoons cinnamon
¾ teaspoon salt
½ teaspoon baking soda

1¼ cups sugar
2 eggs

¾ cup (1½ sticks) unsalted butter, room temperature
¼ cup vegetable shortening, room temperature
1 tablespoon vanilla extract
½ teaspoon almond extract

1 egg
½ teaspoon salt

Combine nuts, flour, cinnamon, salt and baking soda until well blended. Set aside.

Beat sugar and eggs in medium bowl of electric mixer until foamy and light. Add butter and shortening and mix until fluffy. Add extracts and blend well. Add nut mixture and combine thoroughly just until flour is incorporated; *do not overbeat.*

Transfer dough to waxed paper and roll into 2 cylinders each about 14 inches long and 1½ inches in diameter. Wrap well and freeze until firm.

About 15 minutes before baking, position rack in center of oven and preheat to 375°F. Cut cylinders into slices ¼ inch thick, reshaping into circles if necessary. Place 1 inch apart on ungreased baking sheet. Beat egg with salt and use to brush over dough. Bake until lightly browned, about 8 to 10 minutes. Immediately remove from baking sheet and cool on wire racks.

Lemon Cookies

Makes about 5 dozen

1 cup (2 sticks) butter, room temperature, cut into pieces
¾ cup sugar
3 egg yolks

2½ cups all purpose flour
1 teaspoon lemon extract
Grated peel of 1 lemon

Combine butter and sugar in processor or medium bowl of electric mixer and blend until smooth. Add yolks 1 at a time, mixing well after each addition. Blend in remaining ingredients. Shape dough into 1½-inch-thick cylinder. Wrap in plastic and chill at least 30 minutes.

Preheat oven to 375°F. Cut dough into ¼-inch slices and arrange on baking sheet. Bake until lightly browned, about 10 to 12 minutes. Let cool on rack.

Filbert Biscotti

Biscotti can be stored in airtight container for up to 2 weeks.

Makes about 6 dozen

6 eggs, separated, room temperature
2¼ cups sugar
Pinch of cream of tartar
1½ cups (8 ounces) filberts (hazelnuts), husked, toasted, and coarsely chopped
1 cup (2 sticks) unsalted butter, melted and cooled

2¼ teaspoons aniseed, lightly crushed
1 teaspoon grated orange peel
1 teaspoon vanilla
7 cups unbleached all purpose flour
1½ teaspoons baking powder
Pinch of salt

1 egg white, beaten to blend

Beat yolks with 1 cup plus 2 tablespoons sugar in large bowl of electric mixer until pale yellow and mixture forms a ribbon when beaters are lifted, about 6 minutes. Beat whites with cream of tartar in separate bowl until stiff but not dry. Fold remaining 1 cup plus 2 tablespoons sugar into whites. Gently fold large spoonful of whites into yolk mixture to lighten, then fold in remaining whites. Fold in nuts, butter, aniseed, orange peel and vanilla. Combine flour, baking powder and salt. Gradually fold into egg mixture.

Preheat oven to 375°F. Lightly grease 2 baking sheets. Form dough into 7 cylinders, each 8 to 10 inches long and 1½ inches in diameter. Arrange on prepared sheets, spacing 1 to 2 inches apart. Brush lightly with egg white. Bake until slightly springy to touch, about 25 minutes. Remove from oven. Using serrated knife, cut rolls directly on baking sheets at 45° angle into pieces ¾ inch wide and 2 to 3 inches long. Turn cookie slices cut surface down. Reduce oven temperature to 325°F. Continue baking until cookies are light brown, about 20 minutes. Cool on racks.

Poppy Seed Cookies

Makes about 5 dozen

1 cup sugar
Minced peel of 1 orange
1 egg yolk
1 cup (2 sticks) unsalted butter, room temperature, cut into 8 pieces

½ teaspoon freshly grated nutmeg
1 cup unbleached all purpose flour
1 cup cake flour
¼ cup poppy seed

Combine sugar and orange peel in medium bowl. Add egg yolk and beat until light. Add butter, salt and nutmeg and mix until light and fluffy. Add remaining ingredients and mix thoroughly. *Do not overbeat.*

Divide dough into 4 equal portions. Arrange each on sheet of plastic wrap. Using plastic as aid, shape dough into 2 × 4-inch cylinders. Seal and refrigerate until firm, 1 hour. *(Can be prepared ahead to this point and frozen.)*

Position rack in center of oven and preheat to 350°F. Cut dough into ¼-inch slices. Arrange on ungreased baking sheet, spacing 1½ inches apart. Bake until edges are lightly browned, about 8 minutes. Transfer to wire rack and let cool.

Sack Wafers

These crisp cookies are flavored with Sherry, which was called "sack" in sixteenth-century England.

Can be prepared 4 days ahead and stored in airtight container.

Makes about 30 cookies

Butter
5 tablespoons unsalted butter
½ cup rolled oats
½ cup all purpose flour
⅓ cup sugar

2 tablespoons medium-dry Sherry
2 tablespoons honey
¼ teaspoon baking powder

Preheat oven to 400°F. Butter large baking sheet. Melt 5 tablespoons butter in heavy medium saucepan over low heat. Remove from heat and stir in remaining ingredients. Drop by teaspoons onto prepared baking sheet, spacing 2 inches apart. Bake 5 minutes. Cool on sheet 2 minutes, then transfer to rack using metal spatula. Cool completely.

Australian Brandy Snaps

Makes about 30 cookies

½ cup (1 stick) butter
½ cup dark corn syrup
¼ cup firmly packed brown sugar
¾ cup all purpose flour

2 cups whipping cream
½ cup sugar
2 tablespoons brandy

Preheat oven to 375°F. Generously grease both baking sheet and handle of wooden spoon. Combine butter, syrup and brown sugar in small saucepan. Place over medium heat and stir until butter melts. Mix in flour. Bring to boil, stirring constantly. Remove from heat and let stand until slightly thickened but still warm. *Mixture must not cool; place pan in another pan of water (110°F to 120°F) to maintain proper consistency.*

Drop batter by scant teaspoonfuls onto prepared baking sheet, making no more than 5 per batch because snaps harden quickly and must be rolled very quickly after removal from oven. Bake 4 to 5 minutes, until bubbly and golden. Let cool only slightly. Working quickly, roll up on handle of wooden spoon, forming cylinders about ¾ to 1 inch in diameter. Remove and transfer to rack to cool. *If cookies become too firm to roll, return sheet to oven 1 to 2 minutes until they soften.*

Lightly whip cream. Gradually add sugar and continue beating until stiff. Quickly blend in brandy. Spoon into pastry bag fitted with plain tip. Pipe whipped cream into each cookie, filling from each end into middle. Serve immediately.

Cinnamon Stars

Cookies can be stored in airtight container up to 3 weeks or frozen up to 2 months.

Makes about 3½ dozen

⅓ cup less 2 teaspoons egg whites, room temperature
⅛ teaspoon salt
2¼ cups powdered sugar, sifted
2½ cups (12 ounces) slivered almonds, finely ground

1 tablespoon cinnamon
¼ teaspoon finely grated lemon peel
Additional powdered sugar

1¾ teaspoons (about) light rum

Preheat oven to 325°F. Butter and flour baking sheets. Combine egg whites and salt in medium bowl of electric mixer and beat at high speed until soft peaks form. Gradually add powdered sugar, beating constantly until whites are stiff but not dry. Set aside ⅓ cup of mixture for glaze. Gently fold ground almonds, cinnamon and lemon peel into remaining whites. (If dough is too soft or sticky to roll, turn out onto work surface that has been sprinkled generously with powdered sugar. Dust dough with additional powdered sugar and let stand 10 to 15 minutes to dry slightly.)

Dust work surface and rolling pin generously with powdered sugar. Roll dough out to thickness of ¼ inch. Cut out cookies using 2½-inch star-shaped cutter. Transfer to prepared baking sheets. Gradually add 1¾ teaspoons rum to reserved egg whites and stir until mixture is spreadable. Lightly glaze tops of stars, adding several more drops rum if glaze begins to dry out. Bake until cookies are deep golden and crisp on outside but slightly chewy in center, about 25 to 30 minutes. Immediately transfer to racks and cool completely. Transfer to airtight container to mellow for 24 hours; open container briefly before serving.

Gingersnaps

Cookies can be prepared up to 1 month ahead. Store in airtight container in cool, dry place.

Makes about 30 dozen

1½ cups firmly packed light brown sugar
¼ cup blackstrap *or* dark molasses
1 egg, room temperature
1 cup (2 sticks) butter, melted and slightly cooled
2⅔ cups sifted all purpose flour

2 teaspoons ground ginger
1½ teaspoons ground cloves
1½ teaspoons cinnamon
1½ teaspoons baking soda
⅜ teaspoon salt

Granulated sugar

Combine brown sugar, molasses and egg in large bowl and mix well. Beat in butter. Stir in flour, ginger, cloves, cinnamon, baking soda and salt. Turn dough out onto lightly floured surface and shape into 4 long logs. Roll logs back and forth several times. Cut each in half crosswise. Shape logs to diameter of about ⅝ inch. Freeze until thoroughly chilled, about 1 hour.

Preheat oven to 350°F. Lightly grease baking sheet. Pour sugar into pie plate to depth of about ¼ inch. Remove 1 log from freezer and cut into ¼-inch slices. Dip slices into sugar, turning several times to coat entire surface and pressing dough to spread and flatten to thickness of about ⅛ inch. Transfer slices to prepared baking sheet, spacing about 1 inch apart. Bake until lightly browned but still soft, about 6 to 8 minutes. Let cool until almost hard, about 30 seconds. Using spatula, quickly transfer cookies to sheet of waxed paper; *if cooled too long, cookies will cling to pan and break when removed.* (If cookies harden before removal from baking sheet, return to oven for about 30 seconds.) Sprinkle with sugar. Repeat with remaining dough.

Nutmeg Flats

Makes about 32 bars

1 cup (2 sticks) unsalted butter, room temperature
1 cup sugar
1 egg yolk

2 cups unbleached all purpose flour
1½ teaspoons freshly grated nutmeg
1 egg white, beaten

Preheat oven to 275°F. Grease 10 × 15-inch jelly roll pan. Cream butter with sugar in large bowl until light and fluffy. Add egg yolk and beat well. Stir in flour and nutmeg, blending thoroughly. Turn into prepared pan, spreading evenly with fingertips. Brush top with beaten egg white. Bake until lightly browned, about 50 minutes. Cut into bars while still warm.

Sugar and Spice Cookies

These cookies should be stored in an airtight container. They also freeze well.

Makes about 3½ dozen

1 cup sugar
¾ cup vegetable shortening
¼ cup molasses
1 egg
2 cups all purpose flour

2 teaspoons baking soda
1 teaspoon cinnamon
¾ teaspoon ground ginger
¾ teaspoon ground cloves
¼ teaspoon salt

Preheat oven to 375°F. Lightly grease baking sheets. Combine sugar, shortening, molasses and egg in large bowl and blend until smooth. Stir in remaining ingredients. Drop dough onto prepared sheets by teaspoons, spacing 2 inches apart. Bake until lightly browned, about 10 minutes (bake 2 more minutes for crisper cookie). Let cool on rack.

Dentelles

Makes 12 to 16 cookies

½ cup powdered sugar
½ cup (1 stick) butter, cut into small pieces
⅓ cup light corn syrup

½ cup all purpose flour
1½ tablespoons anise liqueur *or* Galliano
1 tablespoon aniseed

Preheat oven to 350°F. Generously butter 2 baking sheets and set aside. Combine sugar, butter and corn syrup in small saucepan. Place over low heat and cook, stirring several times, until butter is melted; *do not boil.* Remove from heat. Add flour and beat until smooth with whisk or electric mixer. Stir in liqueur and aniseed. Mixture will be thin but will thicken as it stands.

Spoon batter for 2 cookies on each baking sheet, using 1 tablespoon for each (they will spread considerably). Bake until cookies are golden and have almost stopped bubbling, 8 to 10 minutes. Cool 1½ to 2 minutes on sheet; *do not remove sooner or cookies will flatten and collapse.* Carefully remove with large metal spatula and slide onto paper towels, folding cookie loosely into fan shape. There should be enough butter left on baking sheets so cookies can be removed easily, but brush or rub lightly between bakings to distribute evenly. Dentelles can also be loosely rolled into thirds or formed into cup shapes.

Tuiles

These delicate almond-studded cookies are sensational with sorbets and ice creams.

Makes about 4 dozen 2½-inch cookies

3 tablespoons unsalted butter, room temperature
⅓ cup sugar
3 egg whites
1 teaspoon vanilla *or* dark rum
Pinch of salt

3 tablespoons unbleached all purpose flour
2 tablespoons cake flour

¾ cup blanched sliced almonds

Position rack in center of oven and preheat oven to 425°F. Generously grease baking sheets; sprinkle lightly with water, shaking off excess moisture.

Using electric mixer *(do not use processor)*, cream butter and sugar thoroughly. Add egg whites, vanilla and salt and beat until mixture is light and fluffy. Add flours and blend thoroughly.

Drop batter by ½ teaspoons onto prepared baking sheets, spacing well apart as they will spread during baking. Using spoon, spread batter into 2½-inch circles.

Sprinkle almonds over each cookie. Bake until edges are deep brown, about 5 to 8 minutes. Remove from oven and let stand 30 seconds. Turn cookies quickly with spatula. Return to oven for 2 minutes. Very quickly press hot cookies, almond side down, in baguette pan, or place almond side up around narrow rolling pin or wine bottle. Cool 10 minutes. Stack together carefully and store in airtight container in dry place.

Lace Cookies

Makes 35 to 40 cookies

½ cup all purpose flour
½ cup sugar
¼ teaspoon baking powder
Pinch of salt
½ cup rolled oats (regular *or* quick cooking)

⅓ cup butter, melted
2 tablespoons whipping cream
2 tablespoons light corn syrup
1 teaspoon vanilla

Preheat oven to 375°F. Lightly grease baking sheet.

Combine flour, sugar, baking powder and salt in medium bowl. Add remaining ingredients and mix well. Drop about 4 inches apart by measured ½ teaspoons onto prepared sheet. Bake until lightly browned, 6 to 8 minutes. Let stand 1 minute, then carefully remove with spatula. (If cookies stick to sheet, return to oven for a few seconds to soften.)

Chocolate-Almond Lace Cookies

These crisp sandwich cookies are best served within 1 hour of baking, but can be wrapped in foil and frozen.

Makes about 20 cookies

½ cup (1 stick) butter
½ cup sugar
1 tablespoon all purpose flour
¼ teaspoon salt
¾ cup (2½ ounces) ground blanched almonds

2 tablespoons milk
1 teaspoon almond extract

3½ ounces semisweet chocolate, melted

Preheat oven to 350°F. Line baking sheets with foil; butter and flour foil. Melt ½ cup butter in medium skillet over medium heat. Add sugar, 1 tablespoon flour and salt and stir until sugar dissolves, about 3 minutes. Mix in almonds and milk and stir until slightly thickened. Remove from heat and blend in almond extract. Let cool slightly. Drop batter onto prepared baking sheets by teaspoons, spacing 3½ to 4 inches apart. Bake cookies, 1 sheet at a time, until light golden brown, about 5 to 7 minutes. Let stand about 2 minutes to firm slightly, then remove cookies from foil and transfer to rack to cool.

Using thin metal spatula, spread layer of chocolate on bottom side of half of cookies. Cover with flat side of plain cookie to form sandwich. Cool on rack until chocolate is set.

Tuiles Lameloise

These spectacularly large, lacy cookies are best when served the day they are baked.

Makes about 15 cookies

½ cup sugar
3½ tablespoons unsalted butter, room temperature
¼ cup egg whites, beaten to blend

½ teaspoon vanilla
5 tablespoons cake flour
¼ cup sliced almonds

Preheat oven to 425°F. Butter baking sheets (preferably heavy or nonstick). Tie 2 broom handles together and grease with vegetable oil, or grease 2- to 3-inch-diameter rolling pin to use as mold for shaping cookies.

Beat sugar and butter in medium bowl until soft and fluffy. Blend in egg whites. Stir in vanilla. Sift flour over batter and fold in lightly. Drop about 1 tablespoon batter onto prepared baking sheet. Spread out as thinly as possible without causing holes into 5- to 6-inch-diameter circle, using flexible spatula or fingers. (Batter circles will be nearly transparent.) Form 2 additional circles, spacing 2 inches apart. Sprinkle top of each with about ½ teaspoon almonds. Bake until cookies begin to brown lightly around edges, 3 to 4 minutes. Quickly remove cookies with large spatula and drape over prepared mold to curve. (If tuiles become too stiff to shape, return to oven briefly to soften.) Repeat with remaining batter, cooling and greasing pans between batches. Transfer to rack when firm.

🍋 Index

Credits and Acknowledgments

The following people contributed the recipes included in this book:

A la Côte St. Jacques, Joigny, France, Michel Lorain, chef-owner
Aubergine, Munich, Germany, Eckart Witzigmann, chef-owner
Nancy Baggett
Nancy Behrman
Susan Beegel
Terry Bell
Yvonne Bendler
June Bibb
Sharon Cadwallader
Judith Carrington
John Clancy
Elyn and Phil Clarkson
Martha Conger
Judi Davidson
Diedre Davis
Déjà-Vu, Philadelphia, Pennsylvania, Salomon Montezinos, chef-owner
Suzanne Delaney
Daphne Doerr
Domaine Chandon, Yountville, California, Edmond Maudière, owner, Philippe Jeanty, chef
Ann and Leonard Drabkin
Alain Dutournier
Ernie's, San Francisco, California, Victor and Roland Gotti, owners, Jacky Robert, chef
Joe Famularo
Marie-Odile Fazzolare
Terry Flettrich
The French Restaurant, Omni International Hotel, Atlanta, Georgia
Robert and Shelley Friedman and Ken and Phyllis Nobel
Paul Gillette
Marion Gorman
Freddi Greenberg
Bess Greenstone
Connie Grigsby
Betsy Halpern
Betsy Hanker
Zack Hanle
Karen Hartman
Bill Hughes
John Hurst
Hyeholde Restaurant, Coreopolis, Pennsylvania
The Jefferson Avenue Boarding House, St. Louis, Missouri
The Jockey Club, Washington, D.C., Paul Delisle, director
William H. Johnson
Sally and Tom Jordan
Madeleine Kamman
Barbara Karoff

Lynne Kasper
Judy Kostin
Louise Lamensdorf and Rene Steves
Cindy Lazoff
Rita Leinwand
Le Napoleon Restaurant, Vancouver, British Columbia, Canada
The Leopard, New York, New York
L'Escoffier, Beverly Hills, California
Faye Levy
Madame Chocolate, Glenview, Illinois
Abby Mandel
Linda Marino
Copeland Marks
Christine McCarthy
Perla Meyers
Jinx and Jefferson Morgan
Moustache Cafe, Los Angeles, California
New Canton, West Reading, Pennsylvania
Adaline Officer
Judith Olney
Marsha Palanci
Carol J. Pascale
Elise Pascoe
Suzanne Pierot
Vicki Pierson
Proof of the Pudding, New York, New York
Robert Renn
Joyce Resnick
David Robare
Phyllis Kasha Rukeyser
Sondra Rykoff
Susan Sandler
Richard Sax
Jack Schneider
Stanton and Helene Schwartz
Marcia Seltzer
Edena Sheldon
Sam and Claire Stein
Swiss Lakewood Restaurant and Lodge, Homewood, California
Karyn Taylor
Barbara and Donald Tober
Doris Tobias
Marimar Torres
Maggie Waldron
Jan Weimer
Linda Wysocki
Janet and Roger Yaseen

Additional text was supplied by:

Norman Kolpas, *Liqueurs: A Spirited Alternative to Dessert, Coffee and...*
Rita Leinwand, *Swiss Meringue Techniques and Basic Recipes*
Faye Levy, *Perfect Custard Sauces, Fresh Fruit Bavarian Creams*
Abby Mandel, *Frozen Fruit Desserts*

Jinx Morgan, *Speedy Summer Peach Desserts, Fresh Fruit and Cheese Finishers*
Jan Weimer, *Tips for Gelatin-Based Desserts, Omelets for Dessert, Simple Frozen Parfaits*

Photographs styled by:

Sandra Learned, food stylist, Allyson Anthony, prop stylist: cover; Apricot Yogurt Ice; Green Tea Ice Cream and Almond Cookies; Tangerine Ice, Avocado-Lime Sorbet, Fresh Strawberry Sorbet; Fresh Blueberry Ice Cream
Edena Sheldon, food and prop stylist: Amaretto Peaches Filled with Amaretto Zabaglione; Red and Purple Plums in Spiced Wine, Poppy Seed Cookies, Raspberry Poached Pears, Marsala Baked Apples
Carol Peterson, food stylist: Langues des Chats, Vanilla Almond Crescents, Cinnamon Stars, Dentelles, Fondant-dipped Strawberries
Amy Nathan, food and prop stylist: Cold Pumpkin Soufflé, Moustache Cafe Chocolate Soufflé; Lemon Soufflé in Lemon Shells; Hazelnut Soufflé with Mixed Fruit Sauce; Perla Meyers's Cranberry Mousse, Crystal Butter Cookies, Frozen Mango Mousse

Accessories information

for cover: Flowers by Floratek, San Francisco, California
Amaretto Peaches: Imported rustic reed fruit basket, glass grape basket with rattan handle, fluted dessert cups and saucers, hand-painted apple dessert plates from Portugal, glassware, linens and flatware all courtesy of Williams-Sonoma, P.O. Box 7456, San Francisco, California, 94120-7456
Red and Purple Plums: All accessories courtesy of The Brass Tree, 9044 Burton Way, Beverly Hills, California, 90211
Apricot Yogurt Ice: Flowers by Floratek; spoon courtesy of By Design, Ghirardelli Square, 900 Northpoint, San Francisco, California, 94109
Green Tea Ice Cream: Flowers by Floratek
Tangerine Ice: Flowers by Floratek
Fresh Blueberry Ice Cream: Flowers by Floratek; thermos and spoons courtesy of Fillamento, 2185 Fillmore Street, San Francisco, California, 94115; bowls courtesy of By Design; linens courtesy of Williams-Sonoma

Special thanks to:

Marilou Vaughan, *Editor, Bon Appétit*
Bernard Rotondo, *Art Director, Bon Appétit*
William J. Garry, *Managing Editor, Bon Appétit*
Barbara Varnum, *Articles Editor, Bon Appétit*
Jane Matyas, *Associate Food Editor, Bon Appétit*
Brenda Koplin, *Copy Editor, Bon Appétit*
Judith Strausberg, *Copy Editor, Bon Appétit*
Robin G. Richardson, *Research Coordinator, Bon Appétit*
Leslie A. Dame, *Assistant Editor, Bon Appétit*
Donna Clipperton, *Manager, Rights and Permissions, Knapp Communications Corporation*
Karen Legier, *Rights and Permissions Coordinator, Knapp Communications Corporation*
Linda Greer French
Rose Grant
Elaine Linden
Mary Nadler

The Knapp Press
is a wholly owned subsidiary of
KNAPP COMMUNICATIONS CORPORATION.
Chairman and Chief Executive Officer:
  Cleon T. Knapp
President: H. Stephen Cranston
Senior Vice-Presidents:
  Rosalie Bruno *(New Venture Development)*
  Betsy Wood Knapp *(MIS Electronic Media)*
  Harry Myers *(Magazine Group Publisher)*
  William J. N. Porter *(Corporate Product Sales)*
  Paige Rense *(Editorial)*
  L. James Wade, Jr. *(Finance)*

THE KNAPP PRESS

President: Alice Bandy; Administrative Assistant: Beth Bell; Editor: Norman Kolpas; Managing Editor: Pamela Mosher; Associate Editor/Cookbooks: Diane Rossen Worthington; Associate Editors: Jeff Book, Jan Koot, Sarah Lifton; Assistant Editors: Colleen Dunn Bates, Nancy D. Roberts; Art Director: Paula Schlosser; Designer: Robin Murawski; Book Production Manager: Larry Cooke; Book Production Coordinators: Veronica Losorelli, Joan Valentine; Director, Rosebud Books: Robert Groag; Financial Manager: Joseph Goodman; Assistant Finance Manager: Kerri Culbertson; Financial Assistant: Julie Mason; Fulfillment Services Manager: Virginia Parry; Director of Public Relations: Jan B. Fox; Marketing Assistants: Dolores Briqueleur, Randy Levin; Promotions Managers: Joanne Denison, Nina Gerwin; Special Sales Manager: Lynn Blocker; Special Sales Coordinator: Amy Hershman

This book is set in Sabon, a face designed by Jan Teischold in 1967 and based on early fonts engraved by Garamond and Granjon.

Composition was on the Mergenthaler Linotron 202 by Graphic Typesetting Service.

Series design by Paula Schlosser. Page layout by Tanya Maiboroda.

Text stock: Knapp Cookbook Opaque, basis 65. Color plate stock: Mead Northcote basis 70. Both furnished by WWF Paper Corporation West.

Color separations by NEC Incorporated.

Printing and binding by R.R. Donnelley and Sons.